T0352359

CARE

PHILOSOPHY: THE NEW BASICS

Series editor: Anthony Morgan

This series provides provocative introductions to central concepts in philosophy. The books are written in a clear and concise way, making them suitable for students and for the interested general reader. The series hopes to speak to the concerns, fears, and aspirations of an emerging generation of readers interested in how philosophy might help frame present-day political, societal, and environmental concerns as well as offer insights into personal well-being and flourishing.

PUBLISHED

Care: Reflections on Who We Are
Todd May

CARE

Reflections on who we are

Todd May

agenda
publishing

First published in 2023 by Agenda Publishing

Agenda Publishing Limited
PO Box 185
Newcastle upon Tyne
NE20 2DH

www.agendapub.com

ISBN 978-1-78821-640-1 (hardcover)
ISBN 978-1-78821-641-8 (paperback)

British Library Cataloguing-in-Publication Data
A catalogue record for this book is available
from the British Library

Typeset in Nocturne by Patty Rennie

Printed and bound in Great Britain by TJ Books Limited, Padstow, Cornwall

Contents

Preface

When Anthony Morgan and Steven Gerrard approached me about writing a book on the philosophy of care, I was immediately drawn to the project. Not only is care a central (but often philosophically neglected) aspect of the human – as well as non-human – experience, but we live in a time where the call to care has largely been sidelined in favour of various calls to arms. What follows is my attempt to offer at least an overview of some of the richness that philosophical thought about care has to offer.

My thanks go to both Anthony and Steven for allowing me the space to write this book and for their suggestions along the way. My former colleague Chris Grau has, as always, been a wonderful conversational partner in the face of a number of sticky philosophical points. My spouse, Kathleen, read the entire manuscript and offered many suggestions that I hope will make the book less incoherent and poorly considered than it otherwise might have been.

I dedicate this book to Kathleen, David, Rachel and Joel. Where would I be without their caring?

Todd May

1

What is caring?

About a year ago I met a self-described surfer dude at a conference. We got to talking, and I asked him the kind of socially awkward question a philosopher who is writing a book on the philosophy of care might ask. "What would it be like for you", I asked, "if all of a sudden you had some injury or developed some condition that barred you from surfing for the rest of your life?" Perhaps knowing that I was a philosopher and therefore to be given significant social indulgence, he didn't seem at all bothered by the question. He told me that it would be a great loss for him; in fact, he would feel as though he had lost a bit of himself.

Then I posed the following scenario. Suppose he had been unable to surf for a long time, but surfing had gone on without him. However, later, all surfing had to stop. It had been outlawed, or the climate crisis had made it impossible somehow, or something like that. Would that matter to him?

He immediately said that it would. He loved to surf, and

would miss it terribly if he couldn't do it anymore. But it would be good to know that surfing was going on, even without him. It would be a real loss to him if it no longer happened. A different kind of loss from the one if he had to stop surfing himself, but still a real loss.[1]

* * *

There are people who are really concerned about justice. Not the "It's unfair!" demand of justice for them, but justice itself. The kind of people I'm thinking of here have what we might call an ideal, an ideal that isn't just about what people experience when they are the object of injustice. Of course, there are different views of what is just. For some people, an equal distribution of social goods is the ideal of justice, while for others it would be merit-based: that is, people getting what they have earned. Still others think of justice in terms of maximum liberty for people to do what they want to do. And so on. But however you slice it, the people I'm thinking of here are people who are concerned about justice for its own sake. Not, like many of us, for the effects justice would have on people's lives, but for the ideal itself.

For people like that, injustice goes beyond how people feel about the ways they're getting treated. Suppose, for example, that the kind of person we're considering here is an egalitarian about justice and they notice that someone is getting less of a social good, say money, than everyone else. Suppose they go up to that person and (okay, they're a philosopher) ask them whether they are bothered about that. And suppose, further still, that the person says they're fine with it. They understand that they're getting less than everyone else, but it doesn't bother them. They're a follower of Marie Kondo who just wants to simplify their life without having it cluttered

2

up with the kind of stuff they might buy if they had more money.

The advocate of justice that I'm thinking of here wouldn't be satisfied by that. There could be a number of reactions they might have. One of them might be frustration at the system that distributed money unequally. Another might be sadness that their ideal was not being met. It's even possible that there could be anger at the Marie Kondo person themselves for not recognizing the importance of an equal distribution. Whatever their reaction, it would likely linger. After all, this isn't just some anomaly in the distribution of goods; it's a violation of an important ideal. The world is a worse place because the ideal is not met – not just because of what not meeting it causes, but by the very fact itself that it isn't being met.

* * *

Here's a common one. My spouse and I have three kids. (Well, they're no longer kids. What do you call your children when they're grown up? Offspring? That just seems weird.)[2] We are very close. When they struggle, we struggle. And, like most parents, we were protective of them when they were young. Once, when I was walking in the neighbourhood with my youngest son, a dog came out and looked as though it might attack. I am not courageous by anyone's standard, but I pushed my son behind me and stood between him and the dog. However, when it comes to supporting our kids/offspring/ whatever, I don't hold a candle to my spouse. She thinks of ways of making their lives better that would never cross my mind. In fact, she thinks of ways of making their lives better that would never cross *their* minds.

Are we exceptional parents in this way? Hardly. Parents routinely protect, support, and care for their kids. It's among the deepest bonds that human beings can have with one another. In fact, if parents don't routinely act in the interests of their kids, we find them contemptible or worse. (Granted, as members of the "helicopter generation", we may have gone overboard with this protection, support, and care business. But you get the point.) When philosophers talk about caring or love, this is the example they most often appeal to as the purest case.

* * *

There are sports fans – everyone knows at least one – whose emotional involvement with the success or failure of their teams is a central theme in their lives. Many of them, if they live in the same town as their team, have season tickets to the team's home games and even travel to away games when they can. They are aware of the performances of many of the players and changes in the team's roster. This does not end during the off-season, either. Many teams – even college-level teams – have radio or television stations that regularly report on team news, speculate about the future, revisit important moments in the team's history, and allow for phone-ins where their fans can reminisce, correct, argue, supplement, or otherwise stay engaged with other people who are fans at that same level.

Watching a game or match with a serious sports fan is often a disconcerting experience, especially for someone who is not as emotionally invested in sports. Of course there are different types of fan reactions, from the shouter ("Yes, yes!", "Oh my God, no!") to the couch coach ("Hand the ball off, you idiot", "Don't put him in; he can't bat against lefthanders") to – and this is the worst – the fan who sits catatonically, quietly imploding until the game or match is over. To watch a sporting event with a serious sports fan is to die a thousand deaths with only the possibility of life at the very end of all that dying. I think it was the former basketball coach Pat Riley who said that in basketball there are only two things: winning and misery.

WHAT IS CARING? A FIRST APPROACH

Surfing, justice, kids, sports: these are only a few of the things people care about. There is also art, for instance. If you're at all interested in literature or art or music, imagine all of the works of Shakespeare or Van Gogh or Beethoven (or worse, Tom Waits) disappearing from the world. You might not even like Shakespeare or Van Gogh or Beethoven or Tom Waits, but surely you would consider that loss a diminishing of some sort, a dimming of the world's light. As well as art, there are animals, pets and otherwise. There is, for an increasing number of us as we become more aware, the environment and its various ecosystems. For some there is mathematics or physics, for others there is poetry or rock climbing. And most of us care about our future and our health.

Caring has many different objects and comes in many different forms. But what is it, and why does it matter? That is where this book is headed. To offer a hint at the outset: caring is in large part what makes each of us what we are as individuals. In a significant way, it defines and reveals each of us in ways that I hope will become clearer as we progress. But to start, we should ask the question of what caring is, a question that will lead us into some thickets of disagreement.

All views of caring, as much as they might differ, agree that caring has two fundamental and related aspects. First, caring involves a sense of the *importance* of the object of care. That

5

is, if you care about something, then it's important to you. Another way to put this is to say that you value it. We might say that to care about something is the same thing as to value it. I'm not uncomfortable with that way of putting things, but I prefer the term "care" in most cases to "value". The term "value" has numerous different uses, some of which might be confusing in understanding what we're getting at here. There are moral values, aesthetic values, economic values, and so on. The term *caring* doesn't have such various uses, so I'll stick to that term. However, if as you read you want to substitute the idea of a person valuing something, that's fine by me.

If caring about something means that it's important to you, then we can see that caring is not the same thing as desiring. I can desire lots of things that I don't care about. At this moment of writing, for instance, I have a desire for a cookie that is in the cabinet behind me. But I don't care about the cookie, and I don't care about having it. As we go through our days, we have many desires; most of them are passing. We might even have a desire for something important, but because it doesn't grip us in an ongoing way, we can't really be said to care about it. To use a contemporary and perhaps uncomfortable example from the United States, many of us are jolted into concern about the seemingly daily mass shootings that have become a hallmark of American culture. But do we care about it? Most of us stop fretting about the impact of these shootings a few days after they occur and don't do anything to prevent further shootings.[3] It isn't, for many of us, that important. We desire an end to these shootings, but don't really *care*.

But couldn't we say instead that we just care a little bit? Don't we care at least a modest amount about these mass shootings, and a lot less but still a touch about having that cookie? In our everyday language we do talk like that. Caring seems to range from passing desires all the way to objects and projects that are centrally important to us and to the people we love. In that sense, caring seems to have different meanings in much the way the term "value" does.

The first thing to note, however, is that the diversity of the ideas of value and those of care are different. Not only can a person value something more or less; there are different *kinds* of values. Some values we might want to call objective: moral values for instance. For many of us, cruelty is objectively wrong and generosity objectively right. So while valuing as an activity may be scalar, that is, a matter of the more and the less, value itself has some very divergent meanings. Valu*ing*, in contrast, is closer to caring, in that it is a subjective matter; it is something someone does and takes its meaning from a person's doing it. To be sure, a person can value or care in different ways, but they are all anchored in the person doing the caring.

That doesn't answer the question of whether one can care a little, but allows for a stipulation that will help us hone in on the way I'm using the term *care*. While we use the word in everyday language to cover a wide range of desires or emotional involvements, I would like to reserve it for things that are important to us, things that we might say, using everyday language, somebody *really cares about*. And, as we shall see more clearly down the road a bit, there is an important difference between what we really care about and what we happen to want or like at the moment. What we really care about – or, in the terms I'm using, what we care about – concerns in significant ways the particular character each of us has. We're defined in good part by the things we care about and not so much by our passing fancies.

This is not to say that there is a strict dividing line between caring and, say, fancying. There isn't. It is a matter of degree, a matter of the more and the less. But that doesn't require us to throw out the distinction altogether. After all, there's a clear difference between red and orange or, for most of us, between good and great, although it would be hard to say exactly where red passes into orange or good into great.

So far, what we've been up to is drawing the distinction between caring and mere desiring as a distinction between what's important to us and what's not. We should also distinguish caring from needing. It's possible to need something without caring about it, although if we care about something there is at least some way in which we need it.

But how can we need something without caring about it? One way is pretty straightforward. We might need something that we don't know about and so we don't care about it. Any parent knows that (a) their kids need good dental health, and (b) their kids couldn't care less about that. That's why getting kids to brush their teeth is such a pain. There were moments in my own kids' upbringing that I thought it a real deficiency in bathroom provisioning that there weren't handcuffs attached to the sink that I could clasp around their wrists until their teeth were brushed.

Sometimes, then, we can need something without caring about it because we don't know that we need it. But it's also possible not to care about something that we do know we need. Having taught at a university for many years, I have met students who need to do well in particular courses in order to get into graduate school or into the career they're interested in, but who can't bring themselves to care about the courses (or at least the grades) themselves. Perhaps the professor is boring or the student is otherwise committed to, shall we call them, social activities. Some students I've met just don't fit into the academic environment, although they would probably be fine in the work world. For whatever reason, they recognize the importance of doing well in courses in their area of interest, but can't bring themselves to commit to them.

Another way a person can know what they need but not care about it might be in regard to health as they age. Some older folks will know that, if they want to continue being healthy, they need to cut back on sugar or see a doctor regularly or start exercising more. But they don't, because they don't really care enough to do so. This example is a complicated one, though. For some, neglecting their health is probably not a matter of laziness but of another need: to let go of some of the ongoing concerns that have characterized their lives. For many of us, life is extraordinarily regimented. We are told what we need to do for our education, our jobs, our health, our child-rearing, even what we should definitely check out on vacation. When we retire from all that, there is something to be said for sacrificing a few years of life for living more heedlessly. Put another way, it may be that for many of us the need for unconstrained living is more important than the need for a few extra years of life.

So far we've been discussing the place of importance in care, distinguishing it from desire and from need. The other side of the coin is that when a person cares about something, there is a sense of *loss* (or potential loss) when it's threatened. This is not difficult to see. If I care about my spouse or my sports team or surfing or justice, I don't want those things harmed. If they are harmed, or threatened with harm, I'm likely to feel one or another senses of loss or diminishment. (However, as we shall see in the final chapter when we discuss Buddhism and Stoicism, it may be that a person can hold something to be important without feeling a sense of loss when it is threatened.) This is the feeling the surfer dude described when he imagined not being able to surf or the end of surfing as a general practice.

This sense of loss can be expressed in many different ways, depending on the object of care and on the character of the person who's caring. It can express itself as sadness or anger or grief or frustration. If the caring is in regard to an aspect of oneself, it can appear as humiliation or shame. If I care about someone who dies, the experience will often be one of grief; while if a treasured object is broken, it might be more one of sadness than grief. Anger can appear when someone I care about is threatened by another person, or my pet is attacked by someone else's pet. These are only examples, though. We shouldn't think that there is a one-to-one match between a particular type of threat and a particular experience of loss. Somebody's dying could elicit anger, if they committed suicide or were careless with their lives or if the person who cared about them is the type of person who reacts to loss with anger.

One thing to notice here is that when the object of care is threatened, the sense of loss is felt to be in the person them-selves. This indicates the way in which caring *binds* a person to what they care about, a point that will be important in the next chapter on care ethics. I care about you; you are harmed and I feel a loss. Moreover, it is because you are harmed that I feel a loss. Our engagement with the world through caring means, among other things, that what happens *out there* has effects *in here* because my caring binds me to the world. I insert myself into the world, and it inserts itself into me.

This does not mean, however, that in caring I am always caring *only* for the other person or object or activity or ideal, and what happens to me if they are threatened is just an in-direct consequence of my caring. Sometimes the loss to me is more direct. Think here of the serious sports fan. Their care about the fate of the team is often tied up with a sense of themselves. If the team does poorly, that reflects poorly on them; *they* have somehow failed. This might seem irrational, since a fan cannot (aside from cheering at the event) affect how a team performs. True, but don't forget the role that superstition plays for sports fans. They wear certain shirts or sit in certain seats or watch from certain bars as long as their team is winning when they do that. And when the team loses, it's time to try a different replica shirt or type of beverage or move to the other end of the couch while watching on television.

For the serious sports fan, in losing one might feel sadness (or anger or whatever) in regard to the team, but also embarrassment or humiliation for oneself. The caring in this instance is both for the team and for oneself. The sportswriter Joe McGinnis in his book *The Miracle of Castel di Sangro* (1999: 3–9) describes meeting someone on a train in Italy where he was traveling to follow a second level soccer team. The person he met was a soccer fan who happened to notice him reading the sports pages of an Italian newspaper and invited him home to watch a championship game between the fan's club (A.C. Milan) and a rival. When the club, which was expected to win, lost, the stranger sat silently for some minutes. Then he described how, when he was young, his childhood home and his mother's sanity was wiped out by a flood in an impoverished part of Italy. And he concluded, "And now this", and walked out. Several days later, McGinnis left the apartment when the man hadn't returned.

One clarification before we move on. We have seen that caring involves importance to a person of that cared about object and a sense of loss when the object is threatened in some way, and these two aspects are related to each other. It's worth noting one way in which they aren't related. I don't care about something *because* I will experience a loss if it's threatened. Caring is directed toward the object of care, not just toward me. I may also feel threatened when the object of my caring is threatened (as the sports fan does when faced with the prospect of their team losing), but the caring is not simply about what I will lose if the team loses; my caring outstrips my own interests. We shall see this a bit more when we discuss the relation between caring and love.

WHAT IS CARING? A DEEPER LOOK

In contemporary writings in the philosophy of care, and especially when it comes to defining the idea of care, Harry Frankfurt is the ur-guy.[4] He is to philosophy of care what Cézanne was to twentieth-century painting. Practically everybody who writes about care takes off from his work. (When we look at care ethics in the next chapter, we'll see a slightly different route, but it is less interested in defining care as in incorporating it into normative thought.) Although, as we'll see, there is disagreement about whether he's got the definition of care right, that disagreement starts from his work.

If, by any chance, you've heard of Frankfurt, it's likely because he's one of the few people in recent philosophy to have had a bestseller. His 17-page essay "On Bullshit", which Princeton University Press somehow managed to turn into a (very slim) book and then somehow figured out how to make go viral, is the envy of every philosopher who ever wanted a real audience. It's also, by the way, a very good "book".

Within philosophy, however, it's his discussion of care that has probably had the most influence. To see what he's on about, let's start from an idea we've already met: desire. In his essay "On caring" Frankfurt offers the example of wanting to go to a concert, which I will update just a tad. Suppose you have a ticket to see Beyoncé and you're really looking forward to going. Your friend got tickets the moment they went on sale and, because you took her cat for a week while she was in the throes of breaking up with her two-timing boyfriend, she offered you one. You've been listening to her music while you exercise and have been dropping her name ad nauseam to anyone you're around for more than five minutes at a stretch. However, at the last minute another friend calls and needs to talk. Right now he wants to talk, just as you're putting on your new limited edition "All Up In Your Mind"-themed hoodie and getting ready to head out the door. He – your friend – just broke up with his girlfriend whom he had been seeing for five years and just bought an engagement ring for and not an hour ago discovered that she was, yes, two-timing him. He doesn't know how he's going to go on.

You really want to see the concert, of course, but your friend needs you, and you do want to help him out. So now you have two desires. Which one will you act on? Your friend really needs you. Plus, the friend that gave you the concert ticket is going with three other people, so you're not really leaving her hanging. You think about these two desires and realize that the more important one is the desire to help your friend out. That is to say, you have a desire to act on the desire to help your friend. This doesn't mean the other desire goes away. It might and it might not; in this case, probably not. But it doesn't carry the day because it's just not as important to you as the desire to be there for your friend. As Frankfurt (1999: 161) puts the point, in deciding to help the friend out, he dissociates himself from the desire [to go to the concert] and proposes to cease being moved by its appeal. He does not merely assign it a lower priority than it had before. Rather, he denies it any position at all in his order of preferences ... The question of whether a person cares about something pertains essentially to whether he is committed to his desire for it ... or whether he is willing or prepared to give the desire up and have it excluded from his order of preferences.[5]

We can see here that for Frankfurt to care about something has a reflective aspect. He tells us as much himself (1982: 260): "Caring, insofar as it consists in guiding oneself along a distinctive course or in a particular manner, presupposes both agency and self-consciousness. It is a matter of being active in a certain way, and the activity is essentially a reflexive one." That is, to be committed to my desire involves recognizing it as a desire and affirming it. That's not all, of course. Affirmation without active engagement is too passive. In some way – or in many different ways – I have to act in accordance with my affirmation if I really care about something.

But does this mean that, for instance, an addicted person who really wants to quit but can't doesn't care about their addiction? When I was younger, I worked for a while in a residential addiction treatment centre. It was one of those high confrontation places that believed that if you just humiliate people enough in their addiction, it will break the addictive pattern. (From what I could tell, it didn't work very well.) It wasn't a pleasant place to get treatment. Most of our clients came because they were offered to go to our place or go to jail. And, I heard, a good number chose jail.

In any event, on rare occasions someone would check

themselves in voluntarily. I remember one guy in particular, a heroin addict. I was preparing his enrolment, and he described to me how he really wanted to get off the stuff, but couldn't. He vividly described the night before he came in. He got a craving, went through the window of a place he'd scoped out, stole the television, sold it, bought the heroin, and shot up. The whole time he was telling himself, "I really don't want to do this". So, knowing that he couldn't control his addiction, he checked into our place the next morning.

Surely, this guy cared about getting off heroin. He reflected on his desire for the drug and didn't want to act on that desire. But he couldn't; he had to act on it. Does this mean that he didn't *really* care about kicking his habit?

We should distinguish here between caring and free will. Addiction, at least in the eyes of many, is a condition where one's will is not free. (You won't see a lot of philosophical approaches to free will that don't at some central point in the discussion consider addiction as an example of an unfree will – or sometimes a free will that parades as an unfree will.) But the fact that he couldn't act on what he reflectively desired doesn't mean he didn't care. Indirectly, he committed himself to his desire to kick his habit by checking himself into a clinic. I could imagine other ways he might have committed himself, for example by trying gradually to lengthen the time between fixes, or by locking himself in a room until the cravings passed. There is no bright line here between caring and not really caring; the distinction between what is important to a person and what is only kind of, sort of, but not really so important is a fuzzy one. But, as we have seen, there are certainly desires that fall clearly on one side or the other of that line.

At this point, let's step back and ask whether Frankfurt's account of caring is a useful one. Should we think of caring as involving a reflective commitment to certain of one's desires? "When a person cares about something", Frankfurt (2004: 16) tells us, "he is willingly committed to his desire. The desire does not move him either against his will or without his endorsement. He is not its victim; nor is he passively indifferent to it. On the contrary, he himself desires that it move him." Is that right?

There are two questions we might ask here. First, is the definition too wide; does it include things as caring that we wouldn't really think of as caring? Second, and on the other hand, is it too narrow; does it exclude things that we might think of as caring?

Is the definition too wide? Let's look at an example. Suppose I'm out to dinner and, having had enough to eat, am presented with a dessert tray that has my favourite dessert on it – a plain cheesecake. Not plain in the sense of only okay, but plain in the sense of being creamy, cheesy, and just a bit loose but without all those toppings whose only purpose is to cover the fact that it's not really a very good cheesecake. Faced with this particular slice of cheesecake, I develop a desire for it. However, I reflect on my desire and decide that I really don't want to have it. If I give in to this desire, I'll feel terrible about myself in the morning. So I turn it down.

Is this a case of caring? Does Frankfurt really want to say that my desire not to give in to the desire for the cheesecake is something I care about? That seems pretty much to fall below the line of importance. Not so fast, though. *Why* do I turn down the cheesecake? What seems to be operating here is a desire to be self-disciplined, which in fact would likely be an important commitment of mine. Depending on how we describe the situation, then, it may be an example of caring. And, in defence of Frankfurt, we might say that underneath what look like commitments that don't rise to the level of caring we may discover deeper and supporting commitments that do.

If we look at things from the other side, asking whether there is a sense of loss if the commitment is threatened, we can see much the same thing. It might seem that a momentary lack of restraint would not cause any real sense of loss, that is, a sense that I lack self-discipline (although those of us in the League of Obsessive Compulsives might beg to differ). But inasmuch as this moment seems to reflect a larger inability to control myself, I would likely face a good bit of self-doubt, especially if an important way in which I identify myself is as a self-disciplined person. (We'll have more to say on the relationship between caring and one's sense of identity in a bit.)

How about the second question, of whether his account of caring is too narrow? Here we meet another philosopher, Agnieszka Jaworska, who has recently argued that, on the contrary, requiring reflectivity in order to be engaged in a bona fide act of caring excludes some pretty uncontroversial examples of caring, in particular caring by really young kids and by people with Alzheimer's disease. In her article "Caring and internality", she begins by offering two real-life examples of what surely seem to be caring. The first is of a son whose mother, because of several untoward incidents, comes home upset about her ability to perform her jobs as both a teacher and a mother, and breaks down in tears on the sofa. The son, seeing this, goes into the bathroom, pulls down a box of sticking plasters, and proceeds to apply them to the exposed parts of her body.

The second example is of a woman in the middle stages of Alzheimer's disease who, among other activities, had always felt it important that she was a master of her kitchen. She now has a live-in housekeeper who cooks the meals, which upsets this woman, making her feel useless. The housekeeper, realizing what is going on but unable to cede the kitchen to someone who would be a danger near a stove, gives the woman small culinary tasks to perform in support of the meal. This makes the woman, at least to some extent, feel less helpless and marginalized.

Surely, Jaworska argues, these are expressions of caring, and it's hard to disagree. The first case, although a single episode, seems to be expressive of the caring relationship the son has to his mother. In fact, it is a classic example of taking care of someone else – although, granted, in a unique way. (Not a less effective one, though. It's hard to imagine the standard hug outperforming the Band-Aids in cheering up his mother.) With the woman with Alzheimer's, the issue is caring about herself and in particular her autonomy as expressed in her capacity to cook for herself. This appears not in a single episode, but in the ongoing relationship she has with her housekeeper and her meals.

On the other hand – and this is Jaworska's point – it doesn't seem in either case that there is sufficient cognitive capacity for a higher order reflection on the desire to help or to be autonomous. The child is too young, and the woman too mentally debilitated. So if we're going to count these as instances of caring, Jaworska thinks we're going to have to abandon the more reflective view that Frankfurt holds and look elsewhere for an adequate account of caring. Where might we look, though?

One obvious suggestion would be to look at people's emotional lives, their emotional engagement with themselves and others.[6] When we think about caring, among other things we certainly think about the ways people are caught up in what they care about. We can see this clearly with the second broad aspect of caring: the sense of loss when the object of care is threatened. This always (or almost always, recalling the Buddhist and the Stoic) involves an emotional reaction of some kind: grief, anger, deep frustration, sadness, and the like.

But we have to be careful here. If we're going to focus on the emotions, it's easy to go too wide. This will require some delicacy in the account. Take for example the "frat star" (i.e. a male, probably housed in a fraternity in college, who thinks that the point of other people, if they even reach his radar, is to serve him) who plays his radio for all to hear at the gym I work out at. Whenever he arrives at the gym, you can feel the emotions of those who are there. We're all tense and irritated, although asking someone like that to turn down their radio is unlikely to end in anything other than unpleasantness. So, in short, there is emotion. But is there caring in the sense we've been discussing here? No. My irritation with the frat star is not important to me, even though it occurs on a regular basis whenever he shows up.

If we're going to look at caring through the lens of emotions, then, rather than the lens of reflective commitment, we're going to have to get clear on the relationship between caring and emotion. This is just what Jaworska does. She begins by offering an account (which she borrows from the philosopher Peter Goldie (2007)) of an emotion itself. Goldie distinguishes between what he thinks of as emotions and emotional episodes. An emotion, for Goldie and Jaworska, is not a single moment of emotional expression but instead an ongoing emotional relationship with the world. As she puts it (2007: 552), "The concurrence over time, of many different interconnected elements, each of which may wax and wane, constitutes each particular emotion". An emotion has different episodes, episodes that involve different thoughts, feelings, states of the body, and so on. But an emotion itself is an enduring pattern of these episodes.

Think here of grief. When we grieve a death, we're generally not sad at every moment. We think of the person we lost periodically, or get reminded of them when we're at a certain restaurant or park, or have conversations in our head with them, or sometimes feel a sadness we can't quite put our finger on, or think of calling them for dinner until we realize we can't. In between these times, though, we focus on other aspects of our lives. We have to figure out which route to take to get to that meeting or what we should do about dinner or why the person coughing next to us on the bus doesn't cover their mouth. Rather than an ongoing episode, grief is usually a pattern of episodes that hang together, in this case because of their object – the person we've lost.

Having the idea of an emotion in hand, Jaworska distinguishes primary from secondary emotions. This is a common distinction in the psychological literature. What isn't so commonly agreed upon is how many primary emotions there are and what they are. Are there two, or five, or six, or eight? Most theorists seem to agree on anger, fear, sadness, disgust and joy. But how about trust, or surprise? However, regardless of how we count them, the difference between a primary emotion and a secondary one is the difference between basic human emotional responses and more complex ones that involve a certain understanding of what's going on around a person.

For Jaworska, a secondary emotion arises when "you understand the situation, when your mental representations (including non-linguistic images) are organized into a systematic thought process that conceptually links various aspects of the circumstances at hand, their consequences, your relationship to the persons and events involved, and so on" (2007:

555). Jealousy, hope, grief, guilt, shame, remorse, and anticipation are some of the secondary emotions. They involve some commerce with the world, some cognitive grip on what is happening or what a person is experiencing. What they don't require, however – and this is key for Jaworska – is a reflective awareness of one's own desires. A secondary emotion can sometimes be about a primary emotion – for instance, shame about being disgusted by a person's appearance – but still, that doesn't mean that the shame requires a reflective commitment to rejecting the disgust. It can be experienced on a less cognitive level.

Now we might ask here, if emotions are ongoing patterns of reactions, are the primary emotions really emotions, or just emotional episodes? It would seem that the automatic reactions we have when we're surprised or angry or fearful aren't patterns of emotion so much as episodes, immediate responses that don't form some sort of ongoing relationship to the object of the episode. I get surprised when I hear a loud noise, but then I realize that it was just a car outside backfiring and so the surprise subsides. I'm not sure myself what to say about this, but we can let it go in any event, because for Jaworska care doesn't involve the primary emotions but the secondary ones.

Care, on this account, is a secondary emotion of a particularly complicated kind. Care weaves other emotions (which have their patterns) into an overall pattern of emotional engagement and response:

Typical components of caring include: joy and satisfaction when the object of one's care is flourishing and frustration over its misfortunes; anger at agents who heedlessly cause such misfortune; pride in success at

21

the object of care and disappointment over its failures; the desire to help ensure those successes and to help avoid the failures; fear when the object of care is in danger and relief when it escapes unharmed; grief at the loss of the object, and the subsequent nostalgia. (2007: 560)

Care, then, is a secondary emotion composed of a number of other primary and secondary emotions. It is an emotional way of being engaged with another person (or oneself, as we'll see in Chapter 4), an activity, an idea or ideal, a team, and so on.

For Jaworska, this account of caring allows us to understand why the young son and the woman with Alzheimer's can care even if they cannot reflectively endorse or commit to their first order desires. They can both have a complex emotional relation to certain aspects of the world (the boy's mother, the woman's autonomy in the kitchen) and are caught up with those aspects in ways that are important to them and that cause them a sense of loss when they are threatened. This also allows her to say that certain non-human animals without a significant degree of cognitive reflective capacities may be able to care – although she does draw the line at a fairly high level: gorillas and chimps could be in, dogs are definitely out. We'll take issue with this briefly in Chapter 3, but for now the key is to grasp the difference between Frankfurt's more cognitivist view and Jaworska's more emotionally based one.

WHY DOES CARING MATTER?

Does caring matter, and if so how? Now that we have a sense – really, two senses – of what caring might be about, we are in a position to ask about this.

There are at least two ways we might approach the question. The first is through an understanding of how our identity is tied up with caring; the second is to ask what we would be like if we didn't care about anything. Regardless of their disagreement about the nature of caring, Frankfurt and Jaworska are in accord in recognizing the significance of caring for who we are as individuals.

We can easily recognize that we define ourselves, and are often defined by others, by what we care about. If you and I get to talking and I ask you about your interests, unless you think I mean just something like hobbies, you're likely to tell me what you care about. In helping me understand who you are, you don't tell me about your weight, your parental heritage, your neighbourhood demographics, what car you drive (unless maybe you really care about cars), your pet peeves, and so on. You tell me about things you care about. Maybe you're a parent, or have a career that matters to you, or you are taken up with learning to write poetry or study another language, or are deeply involved in grassroots activism around the climate crisis. These are the ways you identify yourself, and in turn are identified by others.

We have to be a bit careful here, since this type of identification or definition requires a level of cognitive self-reflection that Jaworska has argued is not necessary for caring. True enough. If you asked the young child who soothed his mother with Band-Aids about his interests, he might reply with a puzzled look. Alternatively, he might answer with whatever came to mind: he likes ice cream and playing with his older brother and watching Sesame Street. Some of what he tells you might be what he really cares about, but that would be a bit of an accident, since he is not at the stage to distinguish reflectively matters that are important to him from matters that aren't. The ability to define yourself through what you care about comes with growth and intellectual maturity, and, as with Alzheimer's, may decline with intellectual diminishment.

Caring also gives us a coherent and stable way of being engaged with the world. Frankfurt (2004: 23) captures this point when he says that, "It is by caring that we infuse the world with importance. This provides us with stable ambitions and concerns; it marks our interests and goals. The importance that our caring creates for us defines the framework of standards and aims in terms of which we endeavor to conduct our lives." Our caring moves us through the world in certain ways; it carves out paths of navigating the world that we take in contrast to paths we don't. If I care about my relationship with my kids, I won't neglect them when they're young in favour of watching all the film noir movies on the Criterion Channel. Instead, I'll play with them, listen to their concerns, teach them what they need to know as they grow older, and – if I'm a helicopter parent – watch over them relentlessly as all this is going on.

In my relation to the world, Frankfurt thinks that in certain instances caring can involve what he calls a "volitional necessity". He tells us (1982: 264), "A person who is subject to volitional necessity finds that he *must* act as he does". When someone is subject to volitional necessity in their caring, any other course of action is unimaginable, at least as a realistic alternative. They are forced to act in accordance with what their caring has willed them to do. This doesn't happen in all cases of caring, but in some. He cites Martin Luther's famous declaration "Here I stand, I can do no other", as an example of this (1982: 263).

We should be careful to recognize that not all caring involves volitional necessity. If it did, then when two types of caring came in conflict, we would be paralyzed, being necessitated to act in contradictory ways. (That can happen, but it's pretty unusual.) Instead, caring has a broadly hierarchical structure. That is, we care about some things more than others, even when we sincerely care about those other things. For myself, I care about philosophy and my philosophical writing. When I'm writing, for instance this book, I set aside time each day to do it and I don't like to be disturbed during that time. I care about getting the ideas right – or at least as right as a person of my intellectual ability can get them. But if, while I was writing, I got a call from one of my offspring (really, I don't know what other word to use here) who had an emergency, I would immediately forget the writing and become engaged with their difficulty.

On the one hand, we can see Frankfurt's volitional necessity at work here. The alternative to attending to the emergency does not enter my mind, and if somebody suggested an alternative at that moment, I wouldn't consider my options but instead just ignore the suggested alternative. On the other hand, however, the lack of a volitional necessity in regard to my writing at that moment would not mean that I didn't care about the writing; it would simply mean that although I continued to care about the writing, I cared more about ensuring the well-being of my, yes, offspring. I would say, then, that what Frankfurt is getting at with the idea of volitional necessity is not the impossibility of doing anything other than what a person cares about, but rather a way of being engaged with the world where particular options for action and ways of being are experienced as compelling and sometimes more compelling than others, even though those others continue to have their own force.

These two aspects of the importance of caring – that we define ourselves by what we care about and that caring carves out stable ways of being engaged with the world – both seem to suppose that we know what we care about. However, we can care about something without knowing we do. In fact, we can even care about something while denying that we care about it. This is because people can – and do – deceive themselves, even about things that are important to them. This is an uncomfortable truth, but one that we ought to face squarely.

Have you ever run across somebody who insists to all who are willing to hear that they don't care about what people think about them? Of course you have. We all have. The point of their saying that, of their making sure you hear it, is for you to admire them as a person who doesn't care what other people think about them. And the fact that they're making sure you know this lets you know that it's important to them that you admire them for being someone who doesn't care what other people think about them. Not that they are aware of all this themselves. They probably aren't. It would be painful for them to know that's what they're up to. So they deceive themselves into thinking that they really don't care what other people think about them.

All of us deceive ourselves about aspects of ourselves we'd rather not see. Among these, some of them may be important to us – things we care about even though, for one reason or another, it would be difficult for us to admit this to ourselves. However, others may not be so deceived. What we care about may emerge through the way we behave, whether it's protesting too much or avoiding certain subjects or exhibiting anxiety in situations where we deny it or focusing intensely on some issue or person we say doesn't matter to us. In this way, what we care about not only defines central aspects of who we are and how we're engaged with the world; it can also reveal aspects of ourselves, if not to us then to others. It may be, regardless of what I happen to say about it, that I care deeply what other people think of me. If so, that will likely come out in the way I move through the world, in what I say, and in how I act with others.

What we care about identifies us, engages us, and reveals us. Let's now look at it from the other side. What would we be like if we didn't care about *anything*?

Firstly, it wouldn't be as though we were just inert or catatonic. Recall that we often desire without caring about what we desire. So we'll still have desires. But how would they work?

Without caring, no particular desire would have a significant grip on us. We would move from desire to desire in a haphazard way, depending on which desire was strongest at the moment. As we've seen, caring introduces stability into our lives, themes of engagement that, because they're important to us, take precedence over other, lesser themes. Without that stability, we would be driven by the strongest desire at a particular moment, buffeted by our desires as they arose one after another. I might be on the way to visit you because I'd like to see you, but on the way I see a pizza place and decide to stop and have a slice instead. It may even be that I promised you that I would stop by, but since I don't care about that (or about you), my emergent desire for a slice of pizza takes precedence. We might even imagine that, as I head toward the pizza place, I remember that I was thinking about going to see that new movie everyone is talking about, so I consult my phone for the nearest movie theatre and head there, leaving the pizza place one sale shorter than it might have been.

Both Frankfurt and Jaworska discuss the way a lack of caring would destroy our ability to commit to anything. Frankfurt uses the colourful term "wanton" to refer to an imaginary person who had desires but no ability to care, and Jaworska refers to an experiment discussed by neuroscientist Antonio Damasio of people who, through injury to the ventromedial prefrontal cortex in their brain, lose the ability to experience secondary emotions, even though they can experience primary emotions and are otherwise perfectly rational (2007: 556). Among the losses they undergo is the ability to plan and coordinate behaviour, which is interesting, since we often think of planning and coordinating as rational rather than emotional. That is to say, they lose the ability to have stable relationships with the world. They become wantons.

Caring matters, then, because it identifies us, commits us, reveals us, and orients us toward the world in stable, ongoing ways. Without caring, we would be very different from the way we are, and in ways that most of us would very much prefer not to be.

CARING AND LOVE

Before closing this chapter, we should probably spend a moment over the relationship between caring and love. There seems to be a natural slide from asking about one to asking about the other. However, we can only really linger here briefly because a full treatment of their relationship would involve a full treatment of the nature of love, and that, as you can imagine, would be its own book.

The number of competing views of the nature of love is legion. In recent discussion alone, love has been seen as: a bond that forms a third entity over and above the people who love (Nozick 1989); an identification with the one loved such that important self-referential emotions like pride, gratitude, and resentment are felt on behalf of the beloved (Helm 2010); an arresting recognition of the rational nature of another (Velleman 1999); an emotional vulnerability to the other that happens in different ways depending on the relationship (Kolodny 2003); a way of seeing the other that involves a particular charitability and offers particular reasons for that charitability (Jollimore 2011); and no doubt others. For the purposes of our quick sketch, we'll stick with Frankfurt and Jaworska, since not only do they have views of what love is, but in addition they have – no surprise – discussed the relationship between love and caring.

For Frankfurt, love is not separate from caring; it is a certain kind of caring. Perhaps the most salient feature of love is what he calls a "disinterested" form of caring. That is, we care about something for its own sake, not subject to an alternative reason such as its meeting our interests, for instance when my caring about a sports team's winning might reflect well on me if they succeed. (Oddly, Frankfurt also thinks we can love ourselves in a disinterested way. We'll return to that in Chapter 4.) We saw a while back that one doesn't care for something simply because one will be hurt or threatened when the object of care is threatened in some way. Rather, care is outwardly directed toward its object. Disinterestedness takes this idea a further step. In love, my caring about the other is more centrally for their sake. My interests might be involved, but they are significantly secondary to my focus on the beloved. If the object of my love is threatened or lost, my grief will be largely outwardly directed; it will be grief on behalf of the beloved itself and much less toward my own threat or loss.

A second feature of love is what he calls the "particularity" of the object of love. What I love is a particular object – be it a person, an ideal, a team, or whatever – rather than that object as an exemplification of something else. I don't love the ideal of justice because it exemplifies a well-ordered world. If that was my relation to justice, it would be the well-ordered world that I loved, not justice. I might care about justice, but only inasmuch as it might lead toward a well-ordered world.

This feature of love opens up a central discussion in the philosophy of love. Does one love a person for their characteristics or for the person themselves? Most (but not all) philosophers reject the idea that it is the characteristics that one loves, for the following reason. If it were only, say, someone's beauty and intelligence that I loved in a person, then if I found someone else with greater beauty and more intelligence, I would naturally "trade up" and love them instead, or at least more. However, that doesn't seem to be the way love works. Our love for our partner is not contingent on someone else with their attractive characteristics in greater abundance not coming along. That other person's characteristics don't move us in the same way as those of our beloved. It is, then, for Frankfurt and for many philosophers who write about love, the person themselves that is the object of love, not simply their characteristics.

The philosopher Christopher Grau has developed some ideas around a thought experiment that helps clinch this point. Imagine, he asks us, what would happen if you were told that your lover was going to die. However, that would not be a problem for you because it would be possible to get you a replacement that was exactly similar to the person you loved.

They would have the same physical characteristics, the same personality, they would be implanted with the same memories, and so on. Would your relationship with this person feel the same as with the original? It wouldn't. That person has a particular history, part of which you have shared with them. You don't share that history with the replica, and it cannot be replaced with an imaginary memory that the replica possesses. As Grau notes, "This is because love often involves, not just an attraction to a cluster of qualities that might be valuable in the future, but a commitment to a concrete individual who has a particular origin and a particular past – in other words, a commitment to an individual with a particular identity" (Grau 2010: 265).

In addition to disinterestedness and particularity, Frankfurt says that love also involves a volitional necessity of the kind we have already seen. One might be able in many cases to choose what one cares about, but with love that often doesn't happen. Love, in that sense, happens to us rather than being something we decide to do. As we have seen, this can also happen with caring, as the example of Martin Luther showed. Moreover, that volitional necessity is a matter of the more and the less – it isn't that everything we love moves our will in an involuntary way. If it did, we could, as we have seen, become paralyzed if we were to love two different objects whose demands conflicted with each other. As Frankfurt (2004: 46) recognizes, "Love comes in degrees. We love some things more than we love others".

Finally, in love, "Lovers are not merely concerned for the interests of their beloveds. In a sense that I shall not attempt to define but that I suppose is sufficiently familiar and intelligible, they *identify* those interests as their own" (1999: 168). This doesn't mean that I necessarily become interested in

31

what interests my beloved. The lover of the surfer or the chess nerd need not become a surfer or a chess nerd themselves. Rather, what is in the interest of the beloved becomes important to the lover in the sense that it is now in the interest of the lover that the interests of the beloved are met. I don't need to become a surfer (thank goodness) or a chess nerd (even more thank goodness) if the person I love is, but it's important to me that they get to surf or play chess.

Love, then, is for Frankfurt a type of caring characterized by disinterestedness, particularity, a degree of volitional necessity, and a taking on of the interests of the beloved. But is this enough to capture the relationship between caring and love?

Jaworska, in an article co-written with Monique Wonderly, thinks not. They offer the example of a teacher whose care for her students is disinterested, who cares about her students as particular individuals, who perhaps would like to care less about them but finds she can't, and who shares her students' interests. Does this mean she loves them? Not necessarily.

According to Jaworska and Wonderly, another element is needed in order for there to be love: a certain type of intimacy. They argue that, "in the case of love, but not mere caring, the individual's sense of oneself as an agent leading a meaningful life is directly compromised without the object and/ or when the object fares poorly" (2020: 11). When one loves something or somebody, its loss damages the lover's sense of the meaningfulness of their own life; their sense of who they are and what they are about is threatened or, as they say, "compromised".

Jaworska and Wonderly seem to have captured an important aspect of love here – at least for many people – but I think something like that is already implicit in Frankfurt's account, or at least that his account would be open to it. As we have seen, whenever one cares about something, there is a sense of loss when that thing is threatened. What the two authors describe here is a particular way in which one is threatened by the loss or diminishment of the beloved. They argue that, "The intimacy of love is a new element, not necessarily present in mere care and this is why it is best not to think of love in terms of a *quantity* of care. A more fitting approach is to think of love not so much as an amount of caring, but rather as a depth of care – or perhaps better – as a way of caring" (2020: 14). This way of caring seems to me to describe a particular type of loss to which a person is vulnerable when they love something. However, as we have seen, the loss that people experience when they care about something can happen in a variety of ways. What they describe here is another way – one peculiar to a certain type of caring – that loss can be experienced. It is, as they say, a deep loss, but it does happen within the ambit of caring and love that we have been focused on here.

2

Care ethics

In the 1960s and 1970s, the field of moral development in psychology was dominated by a single figure. Lawrence Kohlberg, who might even be considered one of the founders of the field, constructed a scale of human moral development that was taken to be the model for understanding the evolution of a person's moral maturity.[1]

His approach was to offer a three-level scale of development, where each level was divided into two stages. The first level is that of pre-conventional morality. At this level there is nothing we would recognize as a moral code. The first stage in this level is that of avoiding punishment. If the child does the right thing, it's simply to avoid whatever penalty their family happens to mete out for behavioural violations: room time, dessert withdrawal, loud rebukes, or some creative means of making the kid feel crappy for having done the wrong thing. This is followed by a second stage in which the goal is not avoiding punishment but gaining praise or some sort of other reward. It's still self-interested, but now the motivation is positive rather than negative. It's about acquiring a good rather than avoiding a loss: candy as opposed to time-out.

Conventional morality is the next level. Here's where most people end up, since they can't or at least don't rise to the level of post-conventional morality. The first stage in this level is interpersonal concordance. Here the goal is the moral approval of others, but it's limited to surrounding others – family and friends, mostly. In this period, the child conforms to the morality of those around them and does so to foster and nourish the connection with those with whom they are in contact. What matters is the local social bond rather than any overarching principles. From there, the person graduates to the fourth stage, that of law and order. Here there is a sense of right and wrong above and beyond personal relationships, but it's a rigid code that doesn't allow of nuance or exception. What's right is right and what's wrong is wrong – and that's the way it is. Maybe because God or my pastor said so, maybe because Immanuel Kant said so, but in any event don't start in with your counterexamples. That will just show that you're wrong.

Post-conventional morality incorporates much more nuance and reflective thought. During the fifth stage of moral development, the social contract stage, personal moral values are integrated with the surrounding social values in order to arrive at a moral understanding that allows a person to navigate a democratic social order with a responsiveness to the needs and values of those around them. This stage is beyond the reach of most folks, as is the sixth, which only a few moral models can attain – that of universal moral principles. This is where a person's behaviour emerges from a fully developed and nuanced set of moral principles that are well grounded in reflective thought. Kohlberg appeals to the examples of Gandhi and Martin Luther King, Jr (perhaps neglecting moments in the private lives of each) as representative of this highest stage of morality.

It would be no surprise that Kohlberg would develop the kind of schema he did, given the state of moral philosophy at the time. For the previous couple hundred years, moral philosophy was dominated by two opposing strands of moral thought: consequentialism and deontology. For consequentialists, the moral rightness or wrongness of an action is determined by its consequences or results. The most prominent consequentialist theory, utilitarianism, argues that what matters in our action is how much happiness or utility results from it. A better act results in more happiness, a worse one in less.[2]

By contrast, deontology is not interested in the results of an act so much as in the means or intentions that are behind it. The most famous deontologist, Immanuel Kant, offered his principle of the categorical imperative as a ground for all moral action (Kant 1997). Roughly, the categorical imperative says that if you're thinking of performing an act, you ought to ask yourself whether you are able to will that everyone in that type of situation would perform the same act. If you can, you should do it; if not, don't. So if I'm asking myself whether to tell somebody who's about to buy my used car about the wreck it was in last year, I need to ask myself whether I could will that everyone hide car damages from people they're selling cars to. Granted, car dealers are not known for this kind of reflection, but to my knowledge Kant is not a guru of the car sales industry.

In any event, at the time Kohlberg is developing his approach to moral development, this is the larger philosophical ethos in which he is working. We might call it an ethos of rationality. That is, for both consequentialists and deontologists, morality is a matter of acting on rational principle. The debate between them concerns which rational principle is the best one. So it's no surprise that Kohlberg's highest stages of morality focus on developing a set of nuanced principles (which, in his case, are broadly deontological) as a basis for action.

Kohlberg's schema of moral development was brought into question (which is a polite way of saying that it was pretty much shattered) by one of his assistants, Carol Gilligan, in her 1982 book *In A Different Voice*. Within a few years of its publication, practically everyone I knew was talking about it. (Had we actually read it? Well, some of us.) It was extraordinarily influential, and continues to be, even if some of its methodology and assumptions are thought to be culturally limited. If we want to mark the beginning date of the ethical approach that has come to be called care ethics, that book is as good a place as any.

What Gilligan noticed is that the tests that Kohlberg was using to determine where people stood morally often had girls and young women at lower stages of development than boys and young men. Specifically, females seem to cluster around the third stage rather than the fourth stage that many men attained. This, she thought, was worthy of reflection. One conclusion that somebody might arrive at here is that women are just not as morally mature as men. After all, they function more on the basis of emotion rather than principle, so wouldn't this lead them morally astray? At the very least, wouldn't it make them morally more provincial than men? But if we wish to resist that conclusion, what would explain this clear lack of moral development?

Gilligan had another idea. Maybe, she thought, the problem

wasn't the women but instead Kohlberg's scale of moral development. Not that there was something wrong with is as *a* scale of moral development. Rather, what was wrong was that he thought of it as *the* scale of moral development. Perhaps there were other types of moral maturity, other *voices* that his approach was failing to listen to here. As she followed up this idea, Gilligan came to believe that women are often on a path of moral evolution that differs from men, not because they can't get as far but instead because the path is a different one. For women, the kind of connection that Kohlberg found at the third period of moral development characterizes not an inferior stage of moral development but instead the roots of another way of conceiving moral relationships – in fact, conceiving them *as* relationships rather than as abstract moral principles.

As a counterpart to Kohlberg's stages, Gilligan offered three levels of her own. The pre-conventional level is self-interested, like Kohlberg's. But the conventional level involves a caring for others, often at the expense of oneself. It is an other-directed morality, one founded on actual relationships rather than abstract principles. In the post-conventional level, care for others and self-care are integrated into a more balanced moral approach.

Gilligan insisted that, although this caring relational approach to morality was more common among women than men, it was available to men as well. There is nothing essential or biological or evolutionary that restricted this approach to women. Rather, it was a product of their social and political history and standing. What was revolutionary about Gilligan's perspective was that it took a set of characteristics associated with women that were typically thought to be morally inferior and instead offered them as a different but equally adequate moral perspective. What has emerged since then is an entire field of ethics that has come to be called care ethics. It is a feminist approach, as we can see, but care ethicists, like Gilligan, reject the idea that it is must be restricted to women. It is an alternative approach to morality, one that is grounded in relationships rather than principles, and, for many care theorists, offers a necessary corrective to traditional moral principles.[3]

WHAT IS CARE ETHICS?

Care ethics[4] is a feminist approach to ethics. To say that, however, requires lingering a moment over the term "feminism". Very few words in recent memory have been so misunderstood and often maligned as that word. Feminism is not so much a set of doctrines as a general orientation that encompasses many and often competing views. For some feminists – although not most care ethicists – there is an essential female nature that has not been respected in most cultures. The goal of feminism, for those folks, is to foster a parallel respect: respect for women's nature as well as for men's. For most feminist thinkers, however, Gilligan among them, many of the differences between men and women are not natural or essential. Rather, they are historical and political, grounded in the different places and statuses that women and men have occupied in most societies. In regard to ethics, men have been associated with rationality and abstraction while women have been associated with emotion and care and relationality.

This, by itself, is not a problem. What *is* a problem is the denigration of emotion and care as ethically relevant in favour of rationality and abstraction. Think here of Kohlberg's view, which places relationships as an ethical matter at the third stage, below where he believes most standard adult morality lies. Views like this relegate women's moral experience to an inferior rank. Now in response to this, someone might say that the real problem is that women have been excluded from exercising their rationality and abstraction because they have been excluded from the public realm where moral rationality and abstraction are practiced. If that's right, the goal would be equal inclusion of women in the realms of rationality and abstraction.

That's not the response of care ethicists. Their view is that the experience of women has its own moral relevance. For them, the problem is not the exclusion of women from arenas where rationality and abstraction are exercised. (It's a problem, of course, but not the problem of women being morally less mature.) Instead it is the failure to recognize that care and emotion are important aspects of morality – for both women and men. If that's right, then the goal is the integration of emotion, care and relationality into ethical thought and action. And that goal requires, among other things, the development of a care ethics, since it has been neglected as part of the general neglect of women's experience.

One care ethicist, Joan Tronto, argues in her influential book *Moral Boundaries* (1993) that in fact care ethics does have some roots in the history of moral thinking, in particular in the sentimentalist movement of the Scottish Enlightenment. For thinkers like Frances Hutchinson, David Hume and Adam Smith, our emotions – our sentiments – of fellow feeling are crucial elements in the development and sustaining of a moral view. Morality arises from the sympathy and empathy we have with others. However, by the end of the eighteenth century, even those views were changing. With the rise of urbanism and a proto-capitalist order, and the social distance that they fostered, sentiment (unfortunately in their view) began to be eclipsed in favour of a more rationalist balancing of competing self-interests. Tronto writes: "What became clear to Smith ... is that as distance increased, the grounds for morality shifted from the concrete and direct approbation of those around us to the less intense but perhaps more reliable notion that, since it was in the interest of others to do so, they would follow these ways of behaving as well" (1993: 49).

As Tronto points out, it wasn't just the changing social and economic order that nudged morality toward a more rationalist path. Women were also making demands for inclusion, and in order to quell them there was a renewed emphasis on women's place in the household, where care and sentiment also belonged (since they no longer had a prominent role in the larger public realm). As a result, women came to be associated with emotion and sentiment while, at the same time, emotion and sentiment – along with women – were relegated to a private sphere often thought of as inferior to the public sphere where a rationalist morality, a man's morality, held sway.

Now it could be pointed out that the relegation of women to the household and their association with emotion has deeper historical roots than the end of the eighteenth century. But that would miss Tronto's point. She's not denying that. What she's saying is that even where a moral theory grounded in emotion and sentiment was dominant (at least for a minute), it declined in the face of changing social and economic conditions. But this raises the same question the Scottish thinkers were confronted with: in a modern world characterized by cosmopolitanism, capitalism and globalization, is there still a significant place for a care ethics? Wouldn't it be better just to recognize the equal capacity of women to engage in rationalist and abstract thought rather than reverting to an anachronistic view of our ethical relationships?

To answer that question, we need first to ask what a care ethics might look like. After all, denigrating an ethical approach before knowing what it is might be considered a tad dismissive. So let's approach matters by asking first what care ethics is and then what relevance it might have in the world in which we live.

At the outset, we might ask what care ethicists mean by the term "care". Unsurprisingly, there are differences in their views, but these differences are held together by the broad idea that the caring they're interested in runs along the lines of "caring for". After all, the caring they're focused on is a care *ethics*. So, for instance, Tronto herself, in her work with Berenice Fisher, says, "On the most general level, we suggest that caring be viewed as a *species activity that includes everything that we do to maintain, continue, and repair our 'world' so that we can live in it as well as possible*" (1993: 103; Fischer & Tronto 1991: 40, emphasis added). Virginia Held, in her book *The Ethics of Care* (2006), sees care as both a practice and a value: "As a practice, it shows us how to respond to needs and why we should. It builds trust and mutual concern and connectedness between persons. It is not a series of individual actions, but a practice that develops, along with its appropriate attitudes. It has attributes and standards that can be described." In addition, "care is also a value. Caring persons and caring attitudes should be valued, and we can organize many evaluations of how persons are interrelated around a constellation of moral considerations associated with care or its absence" (2006: 42).

These definitions are in keeping with Gilligan's idea of caring as a nurturing relationship to others. And regarding the discussion of care in the previous chapter, it might be seen as a species of the broader concept of caring that Frankfurt and Jaworska were honing in on. Although their approaches allowed for various types of caring, they are certainly open to the types of caring that are the concerns of care ethicists like Tronto and Held.

If we turn from the concept of care to the ethics itself, Held offers an overview that emphasizes five characteristics. "First", she says, "the central focus of the ethics of care is on the compelling moral salience of attending to and meeting the needs of the particular others for whom we take responsibility" (2006: 10). Recall Gilligan's view here. What care ethics emphasizes, in contrast to a traditional ethics of abstract moral principles, are particular relationships with specific others. We could say that a care ethics emphasizes relationality rather than individuality, but that would not go far enough. Relationality, after all, can be thought of in abstract ways as well. Someone could argue for proper rules for social relationships that don't refer to specific individuals. Care ethics instead points us to where we live: among particular others, people who have names and faces and, in most cases, addresses.

It would be hard to overemphasize how deep a challenge this characteristic of care ethics is to a traditional rationalist morality of principle. The point of a morality of rational principle is to move *away* from the particular relationships I find myself in so that I can occupy a more impartial position, a position that takes everyone equally into account. For a utilitarian like Peter Singer, it doesn't matter whether a person who is starving is next to me or in Bangladesh; their needs are the same and they should be treated with equal respect (Singer 1972). (It might be easier for me to feed the person next to me, but that's a practical consideration, not a moral one.) For the Kantian deontologist, the fact that I am emotionally entangled with someone is an *obstacle* rather than a spur to recognizing my moral obligations. What I need to do is lay my emotions and my relationships aside and ask myself whether whatever I would be doing for them is something I would will that everyone in my situation would do for everyone in their situation.

At this moment, you might be tempted to ask whether this is really an ethics or a morality at all. After all, do I really need an ethical view to tell me to favour people I'm in relationship with? What, really, is the ethical part of this ethics? This is an important question, one that care ethicists face squarely. It leads to questions of politics and justice, which we'll get to in a bit. In the meantime, let's hold back for a moment while we understand more about what the ethics itself is.

Held's second characteristic of care ethics is this: "In the epistemological process of trying to understand what morality would recommend and what it would be morally best for us to do and to be, the ethics of care values emotion rather than rejects it" (2006: 10). No surprise here. In contrast to the ethics of rationality proposed by consequentialists and deontologists, care ethicists believe that we need to recognize the role that emotion plays in developing proper moral behaviour. Recall Jaworska's example of people with lesions to their ventromedial prefrontal cortex. They were unable to care for anything because they were unable to develop secondary emotions. It's hard to imagine how people like that would be able to act in ethical ways toward others, since they could not have a sustained level of involvement with them. Also, think of the case of the sociopath, someone who cannot experience empathy with another person. (Here in the United States we were recently treated to a very public example of this in the person of our forty-fifth president.) Without empathy, it's

45

hard to relate to the experiences of others and consequently hard even to know how to act ethically toward them (assuming the sociopath would even want to). Traditional ethical philosophy, because it focuses so much more on theory rather than concrete experience, has tended to overemphasize the role of rationality in moral action. Care ethics calls us away from that and returns us to our emotional involvement with others.

Following from the second characteristic, Held tells us, "Third, the ethics of care rejects the view of the dominant moral theories that the more abstract the reasoning about a moral problem the better because the more likely to avoid bias and arbitrariness, the more nearly to achieve impartiality" (2006: 11). What Held is getting at here is not that care ethics is better at achieving impartiality, that is, the idea that everyone should be treated with equal respect. Instead, she is criticizing the idea that impartiality is always better in a moral theory. This may sound strange at first, but think of what it would be like if a person had to be impartial toward all children. That would seem to mean that if a parent had money to fund a summer camp for one of her kids, it would make no moral difference whether she sent one of her kids to camp or the child of some parent she didn't even know.

And when I say that it would make "no moral difference", it's easy to misunderstand this idea. On a traditional moral view, someone might respond, "Of course it makes a moral difference. You're more morally obliged to your own kid than to others' kids. You brought them into the world, so you're responsible for them." From a care ethics point of view, though, that response is cringeworthy. It's not hard to see why. A person's relation to their children should not be one of obligation, but instead one of love. It's about care, not duty. As the philosopher Bernard Williams famously said, if a person has a choice between saving one of two people who are drowning, and one of them is their wife, and they think to themselves that it's okay to save their wife because of their special relationship, that's "one thought too many" (1981: 18).

So impartiality is not all there is to morality. Sometimes it's even inappropriate in our relationship to those around us. Does that mean that there's no role for impartiality? Far from it. But we need to wait a bit before we can address that question, just as we need to wait before asking the related question of whether care ethics just lets us do what we want to do. Both of these questions are about justice, which is also about politics. We'll get there, but not just yet. We need to fill out the sketch of care ethics first.

"A fourth characteristic of the ethics of care", Held says, "is that like much feminist thought in many areas, it reconceptualizes traditional notions about the public and the private" (2006: 12). How does it do so, and why is this feminist? To answer the second question first, the distinction between the public and the private, as it has often been drawn, is one that has several deleterious effects on women. For one thing, as Tronto points out, it tends to place women in the home and men in the public space, and so excludes women from political involvement. For another, it can encourage mistreatment of women at home because issues like rights and justice have been incorporated into the public realm and excluded from the private one. It was not so long ago that men could not be accused of raping their wives, and it is still true that claims of physical abuse of women by their husbands are treated gingerly by public authorities because of the sense of the home as a private space that is off limits to questions of rights and justice.

So, as we have seen, in this reconceptualization there can be issues of justice that concern the private sphere, making it not so private, just as there can be a public need for the incorporation of the kinds of care that have been relegated to the private realm. When we turn to the relation of care and politics in a bit, we'll see why.

The fifth and final characteristic of care ethics that Held discusses is "the conception of persons with which it begins". That is, "The ethics of care usually works with a conception of persons as relational, rather than as the self-sufficient independent individuals of the dominant moral theories" (2006: 13). The idea of people as self-sufficient individuals runs deep in traditional moral theories, and even more so in traditional liberal theories of political philosophy. Regarding the latter, in much of political philosophy the guiding idea is that of the "social contract". That is, in order to ask what a just political order would be, we start by assuming that people are not already in relation to one another. To use the terms of political philosophy, they are in a "state of nature". The question, then, is what would be fair terms of cooperation so that people could join together into a social state? Different philosophers answer this question differently, but they all start from the assumption that people are independent of one another and only later through their own decisions come into mutual relations. (To be fair, for these philosophers the assumption of independence is not a claim about how people really came together into societies, but a methodological assumption to help get the idea of fairness in social relations off the ground.)

What's true of liberal political philosophy is also true of much traditional moral theory. We have already seen an example of that in the case of a parent's relation with their kids. The idea is that we are all individuals without prior relationships with one another, which then leads to the question of what we owe to one another. But, as care ethicists point out, we are from the moment of our birth in a variety of different relationships with a number of people around us. These relationships are not outside of us; they help constitute who we are. Our character is not something we develop independent of our being enmeshed in these various relationships. So, care ethicists argue, an adequate moral theory needs to take this fact into account. Any theory that fails to do so is too abstract, in the literal sense that it abstracts us from our relationships and how they have helped (and continue to help) create us and instead places us in a space that is outside of where we really live and become ourselves.

Care ethics does not fall into that trap. Its reflections take place, not in a realm divorced from people's real situations, but from within them. It asks about our emotional bonds with those around us: how we may understand them and use them in order to develop ourselves ethically in more substantial ways.

CARE ETHICS AND VIRTUE ETHICS

Care ethics is a challenge to the approach of moral philosophy that has dominated ethical thinking for most of the past several centuries. It focuses on particular people rather than abstract others, it values emotion and not just rationality, it doesn't centre itself on impartiality, it questions the public/private distinction as it appears in much of traditional ethical and political discussion, and it recognizes the central character of our relationships with others in forming who we are rather than seeing us as isolated and self-sufficient individuals. It uses the distinctions that have historically been drawn between the masculine and the feminine in order to tease out of the experience of women a way to conceive morality through an alternative ethical perspective.

There is, however, another ethical approach in contemporary philosophy that might be considered as a candidate for absorbing care ethics. Virtue ethics, derived from the philosopher Aristotle, has been offered as a way to place care ethics in a larger ethical framework. It would be worth pausing over this a moment, in order to see the innovations of care ethics more fully.

In terms of philosophical time, which, compared to most fields of study, is somewhat like geological time, Aristotle's virtue ethics is a bit of a newcomer. Or better, it's a bit of a return. For over two hundred years, philosophical morality was dominated by consequentialism and deontology. Then, starting in the 1940s and 1950s, a group of women rediscovered it.[5] Elizabeth Anscombe, Philippa Foot, Iris Murdoch and Mary Midgley were dissatisfied with the state of moral thinking at the time. In the wake of the Second World War and the Holocaust, these philosophers found that approach to ethics to be a bit of a failure to meet the moment, which doesn't seem entirely unreasonable.

However, since (a) they were women, and (b) the field of philosophy has not been an exemplar of how to take women seriously, it was a while before virtue ethics was integrated into the mainstream of moral thinking in philosophy.[6] Now it stands as a third way to think about ethics and morality, a way that owes much to its founding formulation by Aristotle.

Virtue ethics differs from consequentialism and deontology in an important way. While the latter two are focused on the question of how one should act, virtue ethics is more interested in what kind of person one should be. For Aristotle, the cosmos is ordered in such a way that every living thing has a goal or a telos – a way in which it is supposed to develop. Carnations are supposed to bloom with their many petals; cows are supposed to grow up and eat grass and do whatever else cows do; and so on. This is also true for humans. We have a telos, too, and Aristotle's *Nichomachean Ethics* is an account of the human telos.[7]

Aristotle says that the human telos is *eudaemonia*, which is often translated as "happiness", although more recently some philosophers have proposed "flourishing" as an alternative. For Aristotle (Bk 1, § 7), *eudaemonia* is "activity of soul in accordance with virtue", which does make "happiness" sound a touch sedentary. In any event, the broad idea is that for a human life to be a proper one – one that accords with the role allotted by the cosmos – a person needs to develop various virtues, such as courage, magnanimity and friendliness, and express them in their engagement with the world. Ethics, then, for Aristotle, concerns a way of being and not simply a way of acting. There are, to be sure, right and wrong ways of acting in his view. But their rightness and wrongness is more a matter of expressing their character than it is of the consequences or the intentions of the particular acts themselves.

Recent virtue ethicists, although dropping the bit about the cosmos, have adopted the general Aristotelian framework. Instead of finding the human telos to be grounded in the structure of the universe, they find it in more naturalist conceptions of human flourishing, that is, a conception that is grounded in the way human beings are rather than in the idea of a cosmically grounded telos. Although there are lots of different takes on virtue ethics in contemporary philosophy, they all converge on the idea that there are better and worse ways to be human, and that the better ways involve developing certain aspects of a person's character, that is, their virtues.

The question, then, is: is care a particular virtue that should be incorporated into a broadly Aristotelian virtue ethical framework? Should we fold care ethics into virtue ethics as a proposal for how a flourishing life should relate to others?

One source of hesitation here has to do with the view of virtue ethics, particularly as it appears in Aristotle, as individualistic. Aristotle's account seems to focus on the flourishing *individual*; the point of developing virtues is to live in accordance with one's telos. This may seem to contrast with the strongly relational orientation of care ethics. Held, for one, complains that a virtue ethics will "focus on the dispositions of individuals, whereas the ethics of care focuses on social relations and the social practices and values that sustain them" (2006: 20).

This point is well taken, although I don't think Aristotle is so entirely individualistic as all that. For one thing, he thought that in order to develop the proper virtues, a person needs a model, someone they can learn from. Unlike plants and animals, humans don't *naturally* reach their telos. This is because they have something that Aristotle thought (mistakenly, as it turns out) to be solely the province of human beings: reason. In order to reach their telos, then, humans have to use their reason. And among those uses is learning to recognize flourishing humans and learn from them how to flourish oneself. For another thing, he thought that true friendship, in contrast to friendships of convenience or mere entertainment, involves concern for the friend for the sake of the friend, not simply for what the friend brings to one. This seems to me to make friendship the kind of caring relationship that would be welcomed by care ethicists.

Even given these moments in Aristotle's thought, however, it still seems right to say that care ethics offers its own insights into our moral relations with others. I might put the point by saying that care ethics takes moments in Aristotle's thought and puts them centre stage. In doing that, it shifts the ethical ground from individualism to a more relational ethical orientation.

IS CARE ETHICS AN ADEQUATE ETHICAL APPROACH?

By shifting the moral ground the way care ethics does, it might open itself to some criticisms of its approach. It's not as though traditional moral theories don't have their own strengths. They would not likely have lasted so long if they didn't. So perhaps the strengths of traditional moral theories are the weaknesses of care ethics. Let's look at three possible weaknesses: that care ethics is too vague to be a good moral theory; that it can open out onto problematic power relationships; and, most important, that it lacks an adequate approach to questions of justice and impartiality.

In contrast to consequentialism and deontology, care ethics can seem rather vague when it comes to what philosophers call a "decision procedure". That is, one thing someone could want in a moral theory is guidance for what to do in a particular situation. If I have to decide whether to take a job that is morally compromising but will pay me enough so that I can donate to worthwhile causes, it would help to have a moral theory to tell me what to do, or at least to offer some way of thinking this through. If I'm asking myself whether I should tell my friend that someone they respect is making fun of them behind their back, I'd like to get a sense of whether that's the right thing to do. Will I be helping my friend avoid humiliation or violating the privacy of the person they respect? Being told to do whatever caring would suggest is not really going to be very useful. Caring, yes, nice, but really, what's the answer?

Because both consequentialism and deontology focus on particular acts rather than a general moral stance, they can potentially provide prescriptions for how to deal with the real moral dilemmas that people face and for which they want some direction. Granted, there are questions that philosophers raise about whether that direction is adequate, but at least in theory these views give us some sort of guidance. (Frankly, there isn't anything philosophers don't raise questions about. But I digress.)

There are two responses a care ethicist might give to this challenge. First, recall that care ethics is a very new type of moral thinking. Although, as we have seen, there are roots that can be found among the eighteenth-century Scottish Enlightenment thinkers, the feminist orientation of care ethics has introduced new aspects that wouldn't have occurred to Hutcheson, Hume, or Smith. While the consequentialism and deontology that are the stuff of current moral thinking have been developed for more than two centuries, care ethics is only about 40 years old. (By the way, virtue ethics often faces the same complaint and for much the same reason: its focus on character rather than action doesn't provide enough concrete advice for how to act in the face of a particular moral dilemma.)[8]

The other response would be to admit that care ethics doesn't offer a decision procedure, but that that doesn't need to be the point of a moral theory. Perhaps a moral theory doesn't need to be so much about resolving particular moral dilemmas; it would be better if it taught us better ways of moving through the world. And among those better ways of moving through the world, wouldn't caring be one of them, in fact a key one? After all, if we don't care about the people (and not just people) around us, what good will having a decision procedure do? Maybe the best thing a moral theory can give us, rather than situational advice, is a way to orient ourselves in the world that will allow us to be sensitive to what is happening around us. Without that, any particular moral guidance will be useless; with it, the need for particular moral guidance is less pressing.

The second challenge to care ethics concerns its potential imbalance of power relationships. Tronto herself has raised this challenge: "Often care-givers have more competence and expertise in meeting the needs of those receiving care. The result is that care-givers may well come to see themselves as more capable of assessing the needs of care-receivers than are the care-receivers themselves" (1993: 170). This imbalance threatens the autonomy of those who are on the receiving end of care. Rather than helping to build a society of equals, care ethics might tilt into a sort of class distinction between those who give care and those who receive it. Further, it might even lead to potential abuse of power by the care-givers who can come to think of themselves as the arbiters of the central value of care, dispensing it or withholding it as they see fit.

This worry is especially pressing when it comes to the relationship of care and disability. The philosopher Christine Kelly has highlighted this problem. Recounting the potential for power imbalances and abuse of the disabled through a care orientation, she writes, "Care cannot be reduced to a simple definition, and most significantly, the abusive side of care cannot be removed from academic and public understandings. Further, as the disability critiques of care demonstrate, the potential for oppressive care...extends beyond daily abuse to firmly rooted institutionalized approaches to disability" (2013: 789). To counter this, she recommends an approach that she calls "accessible care", one that takes into account the critiques of disability studies in order to articulate a more balanced view of caring between care-giver and care-receivers.

Before addressing this challenge, we should pause a moment to reflect on the challenge's other side. It is often the care-givers themselves that, rather than being the power brokers, are marginalized in our society. Women and people of colour are disproportionately represented among nurses, healthcare aides, service workers, and so on. The more privileged a person is, the more likely they are to be the recipients of care, or at least to be in a position to receive care if they need it. Among the various benefits to be had in adopting a care orientation could well be the recognition of the crucial role played by those whose job it is to care for others, those who are among the central providers of care in our society.

Eva Kittay, in her book *Love's Labor* – written in light of her experience with a daughter with severe mental challenges – articulates a concept of *doulia*. The idea is "grounded in an understanding of ourselves as inherently related to others" (1999: 70). For Kittay, this means that dependence of one sort or another is a universal condition. It does not mean that everyone has the same degree of dependence on others, but instead that we need to recognize the various types of dependencies that exist in a society and be responsive to them rather than thinking of ourselves as isolated individuals that come together into some kind of social contract. In particular, she argues, those that provide care to others also need to be cared for. *Doulia* is the concept of social support and caring for those who provide care for others. Unlike a more traditional liberal political theory that would emphasize our independence, an adequate political theory – and political arrangement – must be sensitive to the various and interacting care relationships that exist in a society and be supportive of them in order to avoid the exploitation of those who occupy caring roles in a particular social arrangement. This, in turn, can address the threat of caring becoming patronizing or dominating. We're all in need of care; the more we recognize that and provide for it in our social institutions, the less likely we are to have exploitative power imbalances, tilted either toward the side of the care-givers or toward the side of those who receive care. An adequate theory of care, then, is intertwined with an adequate theory of justice.

For Tronto, as for Kittay, the solution to this threat of a power imbalance requires thinking about the next challenge, that of justice: "[C]are needs to be connected to a theory of justice and to be relentlessly democratic in its disposition. It would be very easy for nondemocratic forms of care to emerge" (1993: 171). And yet – here is the third issue – how can care ethics handle the concept of justice?

CARE ETHICS AND POLITICS

We have twice seen questions of justice arise in our description of care ethics. In the first characteristic, where care is involved with particular others, we asked how care ethics would approach the treatment of others with whom we don't have close relationships or who are not in our proximity or to our liking. Then, in the second characteristic, where care ethics criticizes the dominance of impartiality in traditional moral philosophy, the question arises of what role impartiality might play in a moral view. These can both be thought of as questions of justice, of what we owe to others – not just to those we're in direct contact with.

In general, care ethicists recognize that questions of justice and impartiality cannot be reduced to a model predicated on caring. But neither can the necessity of caring be reduced to justice and impartiality. As Held writes, "Within a network of caring, we can and should demand justice, but justice should not then push care to the margins, imagining justice's political embodiment as the model of morality, which is what has been done" (2006: 72). If these are in fact two different moral strands, what should their relation be? How should we think of care ethics in a world in which we cannot – or at least should not – neglect our moral obligations to those outside our immediate orbit?

This is a matter of politics. It concerns the place of care ethics in the larger social and political field. Because of this, there is a temptation that care ethicists seek to avoid: that of placing care inside justice, as a kind of a sidebar. Sort out problems of justice and then let care do its thing with what's left over.

This would just return caring back to the very place from which feminist theorists of care have sought to liberate it. If justice comes first, then care is going to be relegated to what has traditionally been considered the private realm – the household in which women (or other care workers) are asked to provide for others through their caring relationships. This is the very picture of morality and politics that care ethics seeks to challenge.

Suppose, however, we go the other way? Instead of thinking of care as a supplement to justice, what if we thought of justice as being built on care? That is, the fundamental moral element would be care, which would in turn support the building of just relationships in the body politic. Would that work?

It might seem unlikely, especially since we have seen how care ethics challenges impartiality and might lead to the privileging of particular relationships. However, let's follow the thread here a moment. Recall first that care ethics, in its feminist orientation, questions the way the distinction between the public and private realms have been drawn. On the one hand, there are issues of justice that affect what has been called the private realm, that is, the household and personal relationships. On the other hand, there is room for caring in what has been designated the public realm. As Tronto tells us, "The separation of care and justice grows out of using the old moral boundaries for describing moral life. But with a different sense of the relationship of how humans are interdependent, how human practices inform human rationality, and therefore how human activity can change what we accept as rational, the relationship between justice and care can be a relationship of compatibility rather than hostility" (1993: 167).

Let's be careful with this quote. What Tronto is saying here is not that justice and care are equal and complementary. Compatible, yes; equal, no. It is care that underlies and informs our concept of justice. Interdependence and concrete practices contrast with independence and abstraction. The place to start is with care, and our approach to justice needs to be informed by care. As Held puts the point,

Care seems the most basic moral value. As a practice, we know that without care we cannot have anything else, since life requires it. All human beings require a great deal of care in their early years, and most of us need

59

and want caring relationships throughout our lives. As a value, care indicates what many practices ought to involve. When, for instance, necessities are provided without the relational human caring children need, children do not develop well, if at all. When in society individuals treat each other with only the respect that justice requires but no further consideration, the social fabric of trust and concern can be missing or disappearing. (2006: 71)

Tronto and Held are not saying that justice and its impartiality can be reduced to care. Their point is more subtle. Care needs to underlie questions of justice. Without care, justice doesn't really get a grip. We have already seen a hint of this in the care ethics response to thinking of morality as a decision procedure. If we don't care about others, what good will a decision procedure do? We can extend that idea into the political realm. For issues of justice to matter, we need already to approach the larger world with a caring orientation. It does no good to ask me what I owe to my fellow citizens or to people who struggle in impoverished areas that are far from me or to those who are oppressed because of the colour of their skin or their gender or disability unless I already think that my fellow citizens, poverty, and oppression *matter*.

Unfortunately, we have an example of a political lack of caring before us as I write these lines. In the US there is, as there is in some other countries, a recent tilt toward authoritarianism, and often an authoritarianism with a fascist hue. (Let's not debate the meaning of the term "fascism" here. In using that term, I mean an authoritarianism that has a racist bent.) Democracy is in trouble. As Daniel Ziblatt and Steven Levitsky (2018) argue in their seminal work *How Democracies*

Die, we're witnessing the demise of two crucial norms that are required for a democratic order to survive: institutional forbearance and mutual tolerance or respect. The rough idea is that people in institutional politics need to recognize those they oppose as fundamentally legitimate players in the field. They don't use every means available to defeat their adversaries but instead hold themselves to moral standards that allow that sometimes they will win and at other times they will lose. Institutional forbearance and mutual tolerance are the normative axles of democracy. Without them, the wheels come off. It's not necessarily violence from without that kills democracies, but instead normative rot from within.

What's worse, however, is the willingness of a large segment of the US population to endorse this anti-democratic movement. After all, somebody is voting these people in, even if gerrymandering and voter suppression are artificially inflating their numbers. And here is where caring matters. Democracy is something that a disturbing number of people in this country don't really care about enough to care for. They care about eliminating the opposition, often with violent rhetoric. And they may call the opposition anti-democratic (although we're hearing less about that than we once were). But the stance that the opposition must be destroyed rather than simply defeated is, in most cases, an anti-democratic position.[9]

Now there are certainly some folks who will argue that the anti-democratic forces in the US do really care about democracy; they're just misinformed. If all you watch is Fox News or other right-wing media, you're unlikely to be aware of much of what's really happening in the world, and a lot of what you are aware of isn't really happening. So you might think you're defending democracy by, say, storming the Capitol, when you're really putting that democracy (flawed as it is) at risk.

On the other hand, however, caring for democracy would seem to entail, among other things, putting in some modicum of effort toward understanding what's really happening in the world around you. To say that you care for democracy but then do nothing to ascertain the facts of the current political situation seems to me to be, shall we say, a bit deficient in the "caring about democracy" department.

But is caring for democracy really something that would flow from care ethics? Isn't it more about caring about particular *people*? I don't see that as necessary for care ethics. If we widen the parameters of caring just a bit, we should be able to see our way toward caring about democracy, that is, having an emotional (rather than purely rational or obligation-based) relation to it that arises in part from our particular relationships with other people and the society in which we've been raised. Recall that in the first chapter (and we shall see it again in the following chapter) we saw that people can care about things like justice. Political arrangements can be the object of care. If we follow Held in thinking of care ethics as involving practice and values, then we can readily see that valuing democracy and practicing respect, tolerance and forbearance can be central to bringing care ethics into politics.

Moreover, as both Held and Tronto among others have argued, care is perhaps the most basic value in a healthy political order. As the case of current US (and not just US) politics demonstrates, if people don't care about the political order they find themselves in, there is no place for claims of justice or other abstract values to take hold. They cannot get a grip on those who do not care about them. This does not mean that those claims and values are reducible to care. They aren't.

They're more impartial and more rationalist. But in order to get off the ground, they need to find their way into people's emotions. They have to matter to people in a significant way and, complementarily, people have to feel their potential loss as a source of sadness or regret or anger or deep frustration.

So, what would a political order that integrates care look like? Of course, it can take many different forms. However, all these forms will have something in common. Tronto has offered a neat summary of this commonality when she writes, "a society that took caring seriously would engage in the discussion of the issues of public life from a vision not of autonomous, equal, rational actors each pursuing separate ends, but from a vision of interdependent actors, each of whom needs and provides care in a variety of ways and each of whom has other interests and pursuits that exist outside the realm of care" (1993: 168). This quote, which echoes what we saw in Kittay's view a moment ago, neatly brings together both caring and justice. Recognizing ourselves as interdependent rather than separate allows us to see our reliance on one another in creating and enacting visions for our lives. This already encourages us to see others as something other than simply enemies to be destroyed. It also presses us to value caring and those who offer it to others. On the other hand, recognizing ourselves as beings whose interests often diverge from one another encourages us to think in terms of justice so that everyone has the opportunity to follow their individual path to creating a meaningful life for themselves. We care about one another and about the political order in which our lives unfold, but we are not reducible to one another and we need to take that irreducibility into account.

Care ethics, then, is not simply an ethics but also a politics. It seeks to integrate our approach to the particular web of relationships in which we find ourselves with the larger social order in which those relationships are embedded. In doing so, it offers a grounding value that, if the care ethicists are right, is necessary – although again not exhaustive – for any interpersonal and political order to be a flourishing one. What began as a protest against the dominance of a particular approach to morality (and, in Gilligan's case, moral development) has, over time, issued out into a larger view of what an alternative ethics and politics might promise for our lives and our world.[10]

3

Care and the non-human

The previous chapter focused on care among human beings. However, care ethics isn't limited to humans. Recall Tronto and Fisher's definition of care: "On the most general level, we suggest that caring be viewed as a *species activity that includes everything that we do to maintain, continue, and repair our 'world' so that we can live in it as well as possible*". The "world" they're referring to includes not just humans but other animals, the environment, social and political systems, precious objects, and so on. In this chapter, then, we'll turn our attention to some of the non-human inhabitants of our world in order to see what caring looks like in regard to them. Let's start with the inhabitants closest to us.

PETS

In our old house we sort of lived with a cat. The cat's name was Sammy, or Rufus, depending on which of our offspring you asked. I say "sort of" because while the cat lived outside on a backyard lawn with a treehouse, we had decided to live inside prior to getting the cat. The reason Sammy/Rufus lived outside was that I was allergic to cats and my family wanted me to keep from having itchy skin and a runny nose all the time. They also respected the fact that I don't like pets. Because they cared.[1]

I also say "lived with" instead of "owned". Legally, of course, we owned Sammy/Rufus. If he had attacked a neighbour or a neighbour's pet, we would have been responsible for the damages. (He was actually pretty chill, so that wasn't a problem. Like other cats, he did go on the occasional walkabout, but that's pretty much it.) If we had mistreated him, we would have been liable under anti-cruelty laws. In short, we were responsible for him and his behaviour. In that sense, he was like our offspring back when they could properly be referred to as kids.

But notice here that responsibility doesn't require ownership. The fact that I'm legally responsible for the behaviour of some creature does not necessarily mean that I own it. Our legal relationship with our children was one of responsibility, but not one of ownership. We didn't own our kids; we were guardians for them. If, in their childhood, they had harmed other people, my spouse and I would have been held responsible for it; and if we neglected them, contrary to our actual helicopterishness, we would have been responsible for that as well. And that is as it should be. After all, when they were young they didn't know better.

But neither did our cat, at any point in his life. Pets don't have the moral wherewithal to distinguish rightness from wrongness, what is morally okay from what is out of bounds. And so, like small children, it doesn't make sense to hold them responsible for their behaviour. Sure, they can be trained to do the right thing, but they can't be convinced to do it. That's just outside their cognitive ken. So, just like small kids, those they live with who can distinguish right from wrong have to take responsibility for them.

None of this, however, implies that it is necessary that we own our pets, either legally or morally. They are creatures that have lives of their own, unlike things we can more reasonably say we own, like sofas and televisions and cell phones. We own those things in the sense that we can, within limits, do what we want with them and people can't just take them from us because they want to use them. Having the practice of ownership of non-living things is, to a certain extent, a good idea. We can question, as Marx did, whether ownership of important social necessities – in his case the means of production – is justified, but when it comes to personal items the idea of ownership has a crucial social role to play. Marx would have had no beef with my owning my comb, even if he himself would have had reason to use it.

In fact, there is reason to consider the relation of ownership in regard to our pets as an unhealthy one. The philosopher and animal rights activist Gary Francione has argued that considering non-human animals as things that can be owned contributes to our general moral disregard for them. He calls our relation to non-human animals a form of "moral schizophrenia". Citing statistics on animal cruelty in sport, entertainment, eating and experimentation, he writes, "We claim to regard animals as having morally significant interests, but our behavior is to the contrary" (2004: 4). This moral schizophrenia, he believes, is grounded in our treatment of animals as property, as things that can be owned. Ownership opens the door to abuse.

Francione recognizes that there are laws to protect animals from abuse. But these laws are inadequate because they allow what is clearly abuse as long as it serves human interests:

If someone kills a cat in a microwave, sets a dog on fire, allows the body temperature of a rabbit to rise to the point of heat stroke, severs the heads of conscious animals, or allows animals to suffer untreated serious illnesses, the conduct may violate the anticruelty laws. But if a researcher engages in the exact same conduct as part of an experiment (and a number of researchers have killed animals or inflicted pain on them in the same and similar ways) the conduct is protected by the law because the researcher is supposedly using the animal to generate a benefit. (2004: 20)

The problem is that non-human animals are not considered to have lives of their own that need to be respected, since they can be owned by human beings and are therefore subordinate to human interests.

The only solution to this, he believes, is to consider animals as persons. The term "persons" here is a moral and legal category, not a biological one. Persons aren't necessarily people. Rather, they are individuals with a moral status that must be respected. "To say that a being is a person", Francione tells us, "is merely to say that the being has morally significant interests, that the principle of equal consideration applies to that being, that the being is not a thing" (2004: 40). Equal consideration here means that, for instance, the suffering of a non-human animal is not less important than the same amount of suffering experienced by a human being.

At this point, you may already be thinking, as Francione does in his article, about slavery. The idea that people could be owned by other people was an invitation to abuse. It was a failure to respect the fact that those people who were enslaved had lives of their own that should not be subordinated to the interests of others. For Francione, the analogy of owning non-human animals with slavery is an apt one, and so the liberation of those animals should follow the model of the liberation of enslaved people.

Here some folks, and among them some philosophers, might balk.[2] The analogy with enslaved people may seem inappropriate, since human beings are very different from non-human animals. It seems demeaning to some to use this analogy, especially since enslaved people have often been likened to non-human animals as a way of seeking to degrade them.

Of course, we may think of this the other way around. Using non-human animals as a way to denigrate human beings can be insulting to those animals. Why should dogs or cows or pigs be a term of disparagement? We have come to think of words like "retarded" as inappropriate because it maligns people with cognitive challenges. Might the use of animal terminology to slight a person fall into the same category with regard to non-human animals?

All of this leads to one of the most stubborn debates in the philosophical discussion of animal rights. It centres on the question of what is called "moral individualism".[3] Moral individualism is the view, as the philosopher James Rachels (1990: 173) has put it, that "how an individual may be treated is determined, not by considering his own group memberships, but by considering his own particular characteristics".[4] It is the idea that animals (including humans) should be treated in accordance with their individual needs and capacities. Different animals, even within the same species, will have different abilities and different needs. We can see this, for example, among humans. Some folks, say with cognitive challenges, will not be able to enjoy certain intellectual activities that might be fulfilling to someone who doesn't have those challenges. They also might have different needs in order for them to have flourishing lives. In accordance with moral individualism, they should be treated differently from people without those challenges.

So far, moral individualism seems pretty uncontroversial. Where matters get sticky is when moral individualists start comparing animals across species. For instance, an adult chimpanzee might have the same cognitive level as, say, a three-year-old human. (I'm using the idea of cognitive level as a basis for comparison, but there could be other or different criteria as well, such as richness of experience or emotional complexity.) If so, then that chimpanzee should not be treated any worse than the three-year-old. In particular, it shouldn't be subject to scientific experimentation or confined to a cage or abused in any way that would be unacceptable to abuse the three-year-old. We can take this idea even further. Suppose an adult is at the cognitive level of a three-year-old. Moral individualism advises us that we should offer the same moral consideration to both the adult human and the chimpanzee.

This doesn't mean that we should treat them in exactly the same way. There may be some things the human might need that the chimp wouldn't, and vice versa. The idea is not that they get exactly the same things but rather that, insofar as their interests are the same, they deserve the same level of moral treatment. This is especially relevant regarding suffering. If you want to know whether you can inflict a particular type of suffering on the chimp, ask yourself whether it's okay to do it to a three-year-old. Further, and more contentious, if you have to choose between inflicting a certain amount of suffering on the child and *more* suffering on the chimp, the moral individualist says to go with making the child suffer.

As you can imagine, moral individualism is seriously controversial, especially in the disability community.[5] Some people take this as a form of disrespect to people with cognitive disabilities. In return, moral individualists take that view itself as a form of disrespect to non-human animals, just as, with Francione, they reject the idea that we can't analogize non-human animal ownership with the project of seeking to own people. However you come down on this debate, though,[6] it does have a lesson for thinking about pets.

At the very least, we should be more like moral individualists about our pets, shouldn't we? We should seek to understand what our pets need, what capacities they have, and so on, and do our best (or at least well enough) to provide them with access to goods that will facilitate a flourishing life for them. Just like our kids, they can't provide these things for themselves, so it's up to us to do it. We don't need to go so far as to claim that we should treat our pet chimp with the same respect that we do our three-year-old. But you get the idea.

Is this because we own them? Not necessarily. We don't own our kids and we need to provide for them. Rather, it's because we are their guardians. By taking them into our household (okay, or in the backyard near our household), we take on certain responsibilities for them. Those responsibilities involve things like food, adequate shelter, affection, room to play, or whatever this particular animal requires in order to have a decent life.

All of this, as you've already guessed, has to do with what caring for pets is about. This is the kind of caring that care ethics was on about in the previous chapter. But it will likely involve the kind of caring we explored in the first chapter as well. It's hard to imagine developing the kinds of relationship with a pet that involves that kind of caring *for* that won't at least eventually come to involve a kind of caring *about*. Whether we think of that caring about in terms of second-order desires or emotional bonds, there will be both a sense of the importance of the pet in our lives and a feeling of loss if the pet is threatened or dies.

I can attest to this personally. Recall that I don't really like pets. My relationship with Sammy/Rufus was, during most of his life, pretty distant. I would feed him when the rest of the family was away, which sometimes instilled in him the illusion that the two of us had more of a bond than we really did. However (although up to now I've kept this from my family, in front of whom I maintained an air of studied indifference), over the years I did kind of develop an affection for the little guy, and near the end of his life was comfortable to take him into the house and let him pad around the place.

In short, although you may or may not be a moral individualist generally, you're probably something close to a moral individualist with your pet. That, and all the affection that it leads to and stems from it, is what caring for a pet is all about.

OTHER ANIMALS

Let's widen out the discussion and ask what caring about animals that aren't pets would involve. We've already looked at one possible take: moral individualism. Let's lay that aside a moment and pull the lens back a bit.

We know that animals are often abused in various arenas: scientific experimentation, entertainment, the destruction of ecosystems, and so on. Perhaps the most egregious daily form of abuse has to do with the activity of eating. We all know this, although most of us would like to put this knowledge aside.

Billions of animals are killed in order that we can have cheap meat on a regular dietary basis: roughly 25 million animals every day in the US alone.[7] And before those animals are killed, if they live in factory farms they're subject to appalling conditions: overcrowding, mutilation, being shot up with chemicals so that they can be fed food that isn't natural to their species. Millions of others suffer scientific experimentation for things like cosmetics and extravagant food testing. Many of us have seen the weariness of horses drawing carriages along city streets or the plodding of elephants around a small ring in the circus or the lethargy of a lion in an urban zoo. None of these animals are pets, but all of them have lives that are subject to egregious conditions through a variety of human practices. What to do?

There are currently a number of curbs being proposed regarding some of the closest relatives to human beings, the great apes. In 2008, for instance, the Spanish Parliament granted a right to life and to freedom from experimental exploitation to the great apes.[8] Recently, court cases have been fought in the US to extend some kind of personhood to chimpanzees, our closest evolutionary relative. For years there have been protests against the scientific exploitation of animals in research. But let's move closer to caring. Given the situation non-human animals find themselves in, how should we think about what caring about them might consist in?

If we think of caring as mattering in an important way and experiencing a sense of loss if the object of care is threatened, then these animals, or at least some among them, might be objects of care. This often happens when people see the practices to which many animals are subjected. The book that is often said to have inaugurated the modern animal rights movement, Peter Singer's *Animal Liberation* (1975), is filled with pictures of animal slaughter. Many people feel that it's the effect of the pictures rather than the standard utilitarian argument he offers that does the real work in getting people to care about what happens to non-human animals. There's a reason it's so hard to get into a slaughterhouse to see what goes on there.

Keeping the focus on food, what might caring about the animals that are treated cruelly in factory farming lead us to do? The obvious candidate for action is going vegetarian, vegan, or at least buying meat only from farms where animals have been raised humanely. (We could discuss the issue of whether the humane killing of animals is morally justified, but we won't. That involves its own complexities.) The caring involved in vegetarianism is not as straightforward as, say, caring about a friend. In vegetarianism, people don't care about particular animals; they don't even know which animals, if any, are being saved through their commitment. But it won't do to say that vegetarians simply care about the *fact* of animal suffering. That seems too abstract. Instead, the caring is something like a caring for animals in general, or perhaps particular groups of animals, like cows or chickens or pigs. The vegetarian cares about them, but in a general sense rather than one that can focus on individuals. The lives of these animals matter to the vegetarian, and they feel a sense of loss or grief or anger or frustration that these animals are being forced to live diminished and often tormented lives. Their vegetarianism is an expression of that caring.[9]

Does this mean that people who aren't vegetarian or vegan don't really care about the animals? Not necessarily. There are several possibilities here. One possibility is that, yes, they don't care. Gustatory pleasure overrides concern for animal welfare. Another possibility, less likely in our age but still it could happen, is that the person eating meat doesn't know about the treatment animals receive in the practices of agribusiness, but would do something about it if they did know. Does this person care? No, they don't, but they would if they became aware. Finally, and most difficult, is the person who can't afford to eat a healthy vegetarian (or humanely raised meat) diet. After all, one of the characteristics of factory farming is that it makes food, unhealthful as it is, much cheaper than more careful practices of farming. What do we say of this person?

On the one hand, it might be that the person doesn't really care about the animals. They're like the first possibility, just more impoverished. They don't have a real choice, but if they did they would still eat factory-farmed meat. On the other hand, though, there are likely people who do care, people for whom the meat they eat is a source of guilt or shame, but they just can't afford to eat a more humane diet. That person does care about the animals, perhaps in much the same way that the vegetarian does. However, they care about feeding their family and themselves more. As we saw in the first chapter, someone can care about two things that come into conflict, where expressing the caring about one precludes expressing caring about the other. Then it's a matter of what a person cares about more. That's where our conflicted meat-eater finds themselves.

There are, of course, other ways to express caring about the fates of non-human animals. Protesting, writing letters to public officials, contributing to animal rights organizations, can all be expressions of caring about animals other than us. But they need not be, just as vegetarianism need not be. Instead, these actions might be expressions of caring about ideals like justice or doing what's morally right rather than

75

about the animals themselves. They might also be expressions of something other than caring, although this seems less likely. It could be, for instance, that a person feels guilty about the situation of non-human animals and is just acting so as to assuage that guilt. They don't care about the animals or any particular ideals, they're just hoping to make themselves feel better by not eating meat or by attending an animal rights protest. As I say, unlikely, but still possible.

It is also worth noting here, contrary to what we saw Jaworska say in the first chapter, that it seems that a number of non-human animals aside from the great apes can also care about one another. Her scepticism about this arises from the emotional complexity she thinks is required for caring. Recall that caring is for her a secondary emotion built on other secondary emotions and exhibited over time. The conclusion that might be drawn from this – and it's her conclusion – is that most non-human animals don't have the emotional architecture required for caring. There are two other conclusions that might be drawn, however, based on whatever evidence might be gathered from animal behaviour. The first is that many non-human animals do actually have the emotional complexity they need for caring; the second is that caring doesn't require that level of emotional complexity.

Let's look at some common examples. Elephants are known to engage in elaborate funeral rituals when other elephants die. Many dolphins work as a team, protect one another from predators, and show expressions of grief; some of them have spindle cells, which are associated with empathy and love. I know of at least one case where a dog attacked a duck pen and a duck stood between the dog and a wounded duck, seeking to shield it. Other animals, such as whales and even ravens, develop long-term relationships with their mates. Although it's difficult to determine what exactly is going on in the minds of these and other animals – and, in particular, whether they have the emotional capacity that Jaworska believes necessary for caring or, alternatively, whether we should revise her account of caring in a simpler direction – it does seem reasonable to believe that the capacity for caring is more widespread than just humans and the great apes.

ECOSYSTEMS

Having widened out the discussion to non-human animals that aren't pets, let's widen out a bit further, to ecosystems. Animals live in ecosystems, which in turn are complex networks of living beings. A rainforest is an ecosystem, as is a lake. Ecosystems can have non-living things in them; certain bugs need rocks to live under, for instance. And the borders between one ecosystem and another are often porous. Is the Amazonian rainforest, for instance, a single ecosystem or a group of ecosystems, since different animals live in different parts of it? The answer isn't clear here, and is probably a bit arbitrary, but our purposes don't require a strict answer. The question we're after is whether and how a person can care about an ecosystem, and so the borders of what constitutes a particular ecosystem don't really matter.

In order to get a grip on the issue, it's worth pausing a moment over a philosophical distinction that will help us sort this out. It's the distinction between instrumental and inherent (sometimes called "intrinsic") value. Instrumental value is the value something has only inasmuch as it gets you something else. The classic example here is money. Money doesn't have any real value in itself. Its only value is as a means of exchange for something else. It's true that some people seem to act as though money has value in itself because they want to have so much of it and don't seem to want to spend it on anything. However, usually the reason for their wanting it is not the money itself but the security or status or flexibility it brings. If they couldn't spend the money on anything, it would be useless to them.

In contrast, inherent value is the value something has, as philosophers say, in and of itself. Its value isn't relative to something else it can get you. It's valuable all by itself. The classic example of this is people. People are said to have inherent value. That is, their value isn't just a matter of what you can use them for. One of Kant's formulations of his categorical imperative is that you should never treat people solely as a means but also as an end. That captures the idea well.

This doesn't mean that you can't use people for your ends. When I go to the store and pay the cashier, I am treating the cashier as a means to my end of getting my groceries. But I'm not treating them *solely* as a means. To do that would be to offer them no respect as a fellow person. At the extreme, it would mean that it would be okay to torture this cashier if it would help me get a deal on the groceries. We have all seen people at stores who seem to be treating cashiers solely as means – yelling at them, for instance, when they make a small mistake or are too slow – but even then, I doubt they would agree that it would be okay to put the cashier to the rack if it would cut the price of their Lunchables, or Pot Noodles.

One thing worth keeping in mind here is that there are things that have solely instrumental value, like money or chalk or a rock to sit on. But I've never been able to think of anything that has solely inherent value. Things that people consider having inherent value, like people, other animals, and, for some folks, art, *also* have instrumental value. They can bring pleasure or knowledge or convenience, and we use them for that. The difference between instrumental and inherent value is a difference between two kinds of value, not a category distinction for two different kinds of things.

It is also worth keeping in mind that what we're after here is not the question of whether the things we care about *actually have* inherent value. It's instead the question of whether in our caring *we take them to have* inherent value. We might take them to have inherent value and be mistaken, either because they don't have the inherent value we take them to have or because there just isn't such a thing as inherent value. That last possibility is another one of those philosophical conundrums that, fortunately for us, we don't have to solve. We already have enough on our hands without it.

The kinds of caring we do for our pets certainly treats them as having inherent value. In the previous section, the suggestions I made about caring for other animals seems to imply that we ought to view them as having inherent value, that is, value beyond their providing us with meat or entertainment or scientific advances. But how about ecosystems? Can we care about ecosystems in and of themselves, not only in what they might be useful for?

Ecosystems – or at least all the ecosystems that I, as a non-biologist, can think of – offer various kinds of instrumental value. Forests, for example, contain all kinds of plants that have various medicinal values. I understand that scientists think that deep in some rainforests there might be undiscovered plants that could help with ailments that we haven't yet created pharmaceuticals to treat. Even deserts can have instrumental value. People have gone to the desert for the pleasure of its beauty, for the experience of solitude, or to test the limits of their endurance. Moreover, we might care about different ecosystems for these instrumental reasons. That is, we care about them because of what they offer us. Their existence matters to us and it would be a loss to us if they no longer existed. But still, can we think of an ecosystem as having inherent value and care about it for its own sake?

Note first that the question of whether we think ecosystems have inherent value and whether we care about them for their own sake are partially distinct questions. We might grant that something has inherent value without caring about it at all. For example, I could not care less about ballet. I've tried, believe me. I had a teacher in high school whom I really respected and who loved ballet. He used to take me to performances and explain the nuances and subtleties of balletic moves to me (fortunately, not during the show). It never took. Honestly, I would be more likely to care about surfing than about ballet, and I can hardly swim. Nevertheless, I am prepared to grant that ballet has inherent value as an art form, assuming art has inherent and not just instrumental value – a point that philosophers of art argue about.

However, although I can grant that something has inherent value without caring about it, to care about it for its own sake implies that I think it has inherent value. I can't care about something as it is in itself and without regard to me and *not* think it has inherent value. Caring about something for its own sake and thinking it has inherent value go together. To see that point, consider this. Imagine that your child or your lover gives you a small keepsake. Kids are always doing this, like finding some basic pebble that they think is interesting and giving it to you as an expression of their undying love. You might treasure that pebble, but only because it represents the child's love. If the child were tragically to die, then you'd probably still keep the pebble. In fact, you'd be more likely to keep it, but only because it reminds you of the kid. Contrast that with the keepsake from a lover. If the lover breaks up with you, the keepsake goes out with the garbage. It has no inherent value, and the only reason you cared about it is because of the relationship you had before they two-timed you with someone else and then broke up with you.

What you care about for its own sake is the child, not the pebble. And to care about the child for their own sake is to think they have inherent and not just instrumental value. If they die, your grief is not just for you but also for the loss of their life, because their life matters in itself. It matters to you *as* something that matters in itself.

So can we care about ecosystems solely for their own sake, that is, as having inherent value? I don't see why not. In fact, there's a term we often use for exactly this kind of caring: wonder. We're all familiar with the experience of wonder. For some of us it happens on a clear night when the stars are out and the universe offers itself up in its vastness to our gaze. It comes to others from the other direction: looking through a microscope and marveling at the intricacy of life. It can arise at the view of a sunrise or flying at close range over a city. It's that warm feeling you get that everything is just as it should be, that this phenomenon you're witnessing gives the universe its point.

An ecosystem can be a source of wonder as well. The beauty of its parts, the harmony of its interrelationships (even though many involve the violence of killing and eating), the intricacy of its evolutionary design: all of these can contribute to a sense of wonder at a dynamic system of living and non-living beings in an often delicate balance with one another. This in turn can elicit the sense that an ecosystem has inherent value, that its value doesn't just lie in the pleasure it offers me but that it is wondrous in itself. Wonder is not self-directed; it's directed toward what engenders it. It's a caring for the ecosystem for the sake of the ecosystem itself, not only for what it excites in me.

One thing to notice here: the kind of care involved in caring for an ecosystem is different from the kind of care involved in loving another person. This difference hinges on the idea of the irreplaceability of the beloved that we saw in the first chapter. In caring for an ecosystem, it is the qualities of the ecosystem that seem to give it its inherent value, while for the beloved it's the beloved themselves, beyond their particular qualities, that does the trick. We can bring out this difference with an example. Suppose that you encountered an ecosystem that elicited wonder in you. Then, later, you encountered another one, a lot like the first one except with greater beauty to its parts, a more compelling harmony to its interrelationships, and a more interesting evolutionary design. (I have no idea how you'd decide this, so just indulge me here.) And suppose that one of these two ecosystems had to be destroyed and it was up to you to decide which one. All other things equal, you'd probably opt for the first one. The second one is more wondrous than the first one; it's like the first one, except better.

Contrast this with the "trading up" issue we saw in the first chapter. Suppose you had to decide whom to save, a loved one or someone else you know who has the qualities that initially attracted you to the loved one only in greater measure. They're more intelligent, more attractive, more interesting, or whatever. You'd certainly save the loved one, and it clearly wouldn't be because of their qualities. It would be because it was them, that person that you love. Even if you were told that if you saved the other person, they would fall in love with you and you'd have a better time with them than with the original person, you'd still save the first person. In love, those characteristics would be entirely irrelevant. Unlike with the ecosystem, the characteristics don't matter, only the person.

In short, whereas in the case of the ecosystem the inherent value would lie in the features of the system itself, in the case of the beloved the inherent value would reside in the person themselves rather than the particular merits associated with them. In both cases, you care about the thing for its own sake and think it has an inherent value. In neither case do you reduce its value to what it makes you experience. But the wonder at the ecosystem is a wonder at a set of qualities it possesses while in love it lies in the beloved themselves above and beyond those qualities.[10]

This distinction becomes important in thinking about issues like the climate crisis. We know – at least those of us who haven't chosen to ignore the issue – that without drastic action in curbing greenhouse gas emissions we are headed for a climatic disaster. This disaster, of course, won't be one for the climate itself. The climate doesn't really care about its temperature. Different temperatures just mean different ecosystems and different living beings. The disaster, rather, is for us as a species, and especially for the most vulnerable among us. Therefore, we are told, we should care about the climate. The state of the climate should matter to us, and if that state is threatened – as it is – we should feel a sense of loss or anger or fear or some other appropriate emotion.

This is certainly right. It's also self-directed. This kind of caring about the climate is a caring for the sake of ourselves rather than for the climate itself. Is it possible to care for the climate for its own sake? That seems a bit off. Climate is just weather over a longer period. If weather is what's going to happen tomorrow, climate is weather over a bunch of years. So it's hard, really, to care about the climate. But it's not so hard to care about what might be affected by the climate crisis aside from us. That is, you might care for the animals and ecosystems that will be damaged as the planet continues to warm. And you might care about them not simply because of what they offer you – food, medicine, pleasant travel experiences – but for their own sake. You might think that they matter in themselves and that that fact matters to you. And so you might care about them for their own sake.

Many folks really do care about the environment in one of these ways: either in itself or in its effects on human life. Some of them care a lot. A whole lot. Enough that this kind of caring has been given a name: climate anxiety. It's the (sometimes paralyzing) fear of collapsing ecosystems, and particularly those ecosystems that sustain human life. If you're young or you have much contact with young folks, you've probably heard about the Gen-Zers who don't want to have kids precisely because of their climate anxiety. Why bring children, they argue, into a world that in a couple of generations will look like a Mad Max movie? Although the tilt of the caring here may be more towards their not-yet-and-maybe-never kids and the suffering they might endure rather than the ecosystems in themselves, nevertheless that caring is bound up with the fate of the ecosystems in which we carry on our lives.

Is climate anxiety bad? Well, when it's paralyzing it can be. On the other hand, if someone has no anxiety whatsoever about the climate crisis and is carrying on as though nothing worth caring about is happening to our ecosystems, that's equally bad. Actually, it's worse. Caring, whether it be for the ecosystems in themselves or for their impact on human and animal life, is in order here if we are to avoid the very worst of the possible environmental scenarios facing us.

So, what should you do? Should you care about the environment as having inherent value or just because of the folks who will have to navigate their lives in the near future? That's really up to you. Whether or not you care about the climate for the sake of yourself and your (eventual) children and grandchildren and friends and so on, or whether that caring extends to non-human animals and ecosystems, the basic approach would be the same: limiting and probably ending greenhouse gas emissions. The point to hold onto here is that there are different kinds of caring tied up with the climate crisis, and so different approaches in motivating otherwise uncaring people to focus their attention on it so that there isn't quite so much sand to stick their heads in.

NON-LIVING THINGS

Care is not only directed to living things or systems of living things. It can be engaged with art, trinkets, and houses, and even abstract things like ideas of justice.[11] Before closing this chapter, it would be worth spending a moment on what caring might look like in these instances.

We've already mentioned the possibility that art might have inherent value. The question of whether it does have inherent value and so, for instance, would have value even if there were no human beings to experience it, is a long-standing one in the philosophy of art. However, that isn't our question. Our question isn't about whether art actually has inherent value; instead it has to do with the relation of caring to *ascribing* inherent value. In caring about art, is it possible that someone could care for a work of art for its own sake and in that way ascribes an inherent value to it?

That certainly seems possible, doesn't it? Take your favourite painter, say Van Gogh or Rembrandt or whoever you like, and imagine that the human race went extinct (remember the climate crisis, head in the sand, and so on) but that their paintings still existed. Might you think that the world was a better place because those paintings were still there, even though there was nobody to appreciate them? I don't see why not. It's not that you would necessarily think that, but it isn't unreasonable. You could just think that those paintings added a certain beauty to the world, just as certain ecosystems seem wondrous in themselves. It might be a shame there was no one around to take that beauty in, but that wouldn't subtract from the beauty of the paintings themselves.

How about if we went further, using an example that sometimes crops up in philosophical discussion: a watch bequeathed by your grandfather? Might you care about that for its own sake? This is a little more complicated, I think. We need to disentangle a few threads here. First, when we think of a watch like this, we often imagine something expensive like a pocket watch that is intricate in design with delicate carvings on its case, a long gold chain, and so on. If we do that, however, we would be in danger of confusing two issues: the beauty of the watch as a work of art and its meaning for you as a gift from your grandfather. The first issue goes back to what we just talked about. So let's focus on the second.

To get a grip on it, imagine a different kind of watch. Imagine that your grandfather, not being particularly wealthy or particularly attuned to good watches, thoughtfully bequeathed you a Mickey Mouse watch. You're not insulted by this; grandpa was just the kind of person who would think a Mickey Mouse watch was just, as he would put it, the cat's pajamas. So you're grateful to have it. But would you think it had inherent value? Here's where things are a bit sticky. On the one hand, you might think that it doesn't, because, well, it's a Mickey Mouse watch and there are zillions of them floating around various kids' bedrooms. However, this particular Mickey Mouse watch is one your grandfather gave you. It's not as though you could just throw it away and pick up another one and it would be the same thing. This particular Mickey Mouse watch, although not really unique, is irreplaceable. It's just like the pebble we saw in the previous section when we were distinguishing inherent from instrumental value. It's not that you think the watch has an inherent value – if your grandfather hadn't bequeathed it, you'd likely toss it or at best donate it to a charity store. To put it another way, you don't care about it for its own sake. Instead, it's valuable to you because it's the particular watch your grandfather, for his own inimitable reasons, thought you should have. You treasure it because it was his and he wanted you to have it.

We can see, then, that, in addition to caring about things solely for their instrumental value, people can care about things in themselves as having inherent value or, alternatively, care about them as irreplaceable even if they don't think they have inherent value. And in addition to material things, people can also care about ideas. We saw something like this at the beginning of the book with the example of the person who cared about justice. They didn't just care about justice as it affected people, but justice as an ideal in itself. I say "something like this" because it's not entirely clear that the person thought of this just as an idea. It could be that they thought of it as a particular social arrangement, and so cared about it in that way. That is, they thought of it as an ideal rather than an idea.

A cleaner example would be the mathematician who cares about the arrangement of numbers. We can imagine a mathematician grieving over the discovery of Gödel's incompleteness theorem, which says that you can have certain mathematical systems where some of its statements are unprovable given the system's axioms. (Please don't ask me for an illustration here.) For this mathematician, the incompleteness of a system would destroy its beauty, undo the architectural balance of theorems and their relationship to one another. It would be like someone smearing mud on the canvas of a beautiful painting. We would say of this person that they cared about mathematical systems in themselves and not just as a way to, say, make sure they're getting the right change at the store. So yes, people can care about ideas for their own sake as well as actual things.

So far we've seen a variety of ways of caring, from caring about things in their relation to us to caring about things in themselves to loving things. And we've seen a variety of objects of caring from other people to non-human animals to things to ideas. But we seem to have left something out: us. What would our caring about ourselves look like? Let's see.

4

Caring for ourselves

If I had a dollar for every self-care book on the market, I'd be standing on a street corner handing this book out for free.[1] There are thousands and thousands of them: emotional, spiritual, mindful, mental, health; for men, women, people with ADHD, people without ADHD, people who overthink, people who underthink, people with immature parents, people with substance abuse problems, narcissistic people, teenagers, dummies, breastfeeders, cats; there is even witch-craft for self-care, which, okay, is kind of intriguing.

This chapter isn't going to offer a bunch of advice about how to take care of yourself. (I'm hardly the person to do that.) Instead, it will consider one thinker's suggestion for a way to think about our lives as a whole. But mostly it's inter-ested in the place of self-care in philosophy: how it looks, what role it has, how we might think about it. We'll start with the place of self-care in traditional moral theories, then turn again to Harry Frankfurt and his interesting suggestion that self-love is the purest form of love, and finally to a historical view of self-care offered by the philosopher and historian Michel Foucault.

SELF-CARE (?) IN THE BIG THREE

All three traditional Western moral theories – consequential-ism, deontology, virtue ethics – offer a moral allowance for a person to look after themselves. Whether we would want to call these moral places "self-care" is another issue, one we'll look into as we canvas each theory. None of them, however, require complete self-sacrifice in the name of moral rectitude. Morality isn't, in these views, just about altruism, although in the end they're all pretty stringent.[2]

Consequentialism, especially in its most common form of utilitarianism, says that your interests don't count any more than anyone else's. But they don't count for any less, either. Recall that consequentialism is interested in the results, or consequences, of an act. In its most popular utilitarian version, it focuses on happiness. More happiness, better; less happiness, worse. This is easy to misunderstand. More happiness doesn't mean happiness for more people. It just means more total happiness. So if you have a choice between creating a lot of happiness for one person or a little happiness for several people, and if the happiness of that one person outweighs the happiness of the others, then you should promote the happiness of the one person. (How happiness is measured is a whole different problem, one that economists and decision theorists try to tackle.)

What this means for me and my happiness is that it's part of the package when I'm asking myself what to do. I can't count it as more than anyone else's happiness (as in, your happiness is worth X and my happiness is worth 2X), which is what a lot of us do when we're thinking about how to act. But I do get to count it. If the choice, for instance, is between saving my life and preventing you and your friend from getting broken legs, then I am allowed to save my life. In fact, the utilitarian claim is even a bit stronger. Not only am I allowed to save my life: it would be the best thing to do. Why? Because saving my life will (presumably) cause the best consequences, that is, more happiness. On the other hand, if the choice is between saving my life or sacrificing it to save two other lives, then I'm out of luck.

What does this mean for taking care of myself? Well, on the one hand, it certainly carves out a space for my own happiness. But there are two other hands as well. On the first of these, it seems to make fostering my happiness more a matter of what is the best thing to do rather than just giving me permission to do it if I want to. If I would rather create less overall happiness by willingly sacrificing myself for something that's important to me, I'm cheating utilitarian-wise. The second of those other hands is more pressing for the idea of caring for ourselves. When we think of taking care of ourselves, we usually think a little more widely than just being happy. Self-care can involve a multitude of things, which is one reason the popular books on it are so varied in their themes, objects and methods. Next to the entire realm of self-care, happiness can feel a bit flat. If you ask me how to take care of myself, and my answer is "Be happy", you would rightfully feel a bit short-changed.[3]

Kant's view is, unsurprisingly, more about obligation than anything else. For Kant, we have duties of self-development, whether we like it or not. Among these duties is to develop our talents. This stems from the categorical imperative. To see why, we need to distinguish perfect duties from imperfect duties. For instance, people have a duty not to lie because, if everyone lied, lying would lose its point. Nobody would believe anyone else, so what would be gained by lying? Kant calls the obligation not to lie a "perfect duty". This is because imagining a world in which everyone lies would contradict my own project of lying. It would make my lying impossible to carry out. In that sense, lying as a universal law is self-contradictory. But not all duties for Kant are perfect duties. Imperfect duties don't involve that kind of contradiction. They involve a different kind of contradiction. Suppose I am thinking that I would rather not develop my talents. Let me then imagine a world in which nobody developed their talents. It's not that it's impossible for me to leave my talents undeveloped in a world like that; leaving my talents undeveloped could still be carried out successfully, unlike lying. However, I really wouldn't *want* to live in a world in which nobody developed their talents. A world like that would be impoverished: no art, no sports, no science, no engagement with nature, and so on.

Developing my talents, then, is a Kantian duty, albeit an imperfect one. It's not the only duty I have to myself, but it will do for our purposes. Like everything else in Kant's moral philosophy, self-development isn't so much a matter of self-care as it is of self-*obligation*. It's a duty; it's heavy. We're not simply permitted to develop our talents; we're obliged to. It's a requirement. We have obligations to ourselves just as we have obligations to others. Unlike utilitarianism, which substitutes the thinner concept of happiness for self-care, Kant can offer a richer account – developing your talents, after all, can involve a lot of different engagements in a variety of activities. But it comes off less as a way of taking care of ourselves and more as a way of living up to what we're supposed to be. Which, for Kant, it is.

This leaves virtue ethics which, as we saw in the second chapter, has affinities with care ethics, and indeed does involve a richer concept of self-care. This might seem strange at first. After all, isn't cultivating and developing our virtues a lot like developing our talents, where that's not just something we're allowed to do but something we're actually supposed to do? This is true, but it can also be misleading. For Aristotle, as we saw, becoming virtuous is the best kind of life for a human being. It is what a flourishing life, a life of *eudaemonia*, consists in. The virtuous person is not only someone who is living up to the human telos, to what a human being ought to be. They are also living a flourishing life. Aristotle contrasts the happiness of mere brutes with human happiness. Human happiness is richer and more fulfilling since it involves not only pleasures of the body but also pleasures of the rational soul, which he thought only human beings have. To attain human happiness, however, requires habituating oneself to the virtues. It's work; it doesn't just happen.

For Aristotle, there is no distinction between self-care and being virtuous. Becoming virtuous is how a person best takes care of themselves. Later virtue theorists, while jettisoning Aristotle's idea that every living thing has a cosmic telos, retained the idea that there is a way to flourish as a human being and that living virtuously was that way. For them, living virtuously conformed to what we might think of as a natural telos – the best way to be a human being. In this sense, what worried care ethicists – that Aristotle's view was too self-directed and not relational enough – is also what allows him to develop a rich concept of self-care.

Rich, but narrow. Since the virtue ethicists think of caring for oneself as developing one's virtues, they neglect aspects of self-care that would be outside the moral realm. Learning a language, meditating, participating in a bowling league, reading a trashy novel, creating a fantasy football team, fixing the perfect Old Fashioned, playing charades with friends, watching the sun set over the beach: none of these are necessarily virtue-cultivating. And if any of them are, their worth lies only as a means to cultivate virtue rather than being important forms of a person's caring for themselves on their own. What we might want to call a flourishing life can't, for most of us, be reduced to ethical categories, no matter how wide we reasonably draw the ethical circle. To be sure, caring for oneself involves ethics, and may at times even involve obligation. (There is a whole debate in philosophy about whether Kant is right in saying that we have obligations to ourselves.) But it can't be just about that. There must be more.

FRANKFURT ON SELF-LOVE

Harry Frankfurt, our philosopher of care from the first chapter, has an interesting view of loving oneself. Although, as we've seen, the question of exactly what love is is a vexed one; for Frankfurt love is clearly a species of care, a particular one that has four characteristics. First, it is disinterested; it cares about its object for its own sake. Second, it is particular; it is love for that particular object rather than simply for a set of qualities that the object possesses. Third, it has a "volitional necessity"; it isn't chosen so much at it chooses. It precludes acting against the interests of the beloved. Fourth, it involves identification; the interests of the beloved are now one's own interests. This doesn't happen in the sense that, say, I become interested in surfing because the person I love does. Rather, surfing becomes something that matters to me on their behalf, because it matters to them.

On the basis of this view of love, Frankfurt makes an astounding claim: "Given these as the defining features of love, it is apparent that self-love – notwithstanding its questionable reputation – is in a certain way the purest of all modes of love" (2004: 80). He immediately follows with this: "The reader is perhaps likely to presume that I cannot possibly mean this". Indeed. How could loving myself be more pure than loving my spouse or my child? That seems ridiculous.

Here Frankfurt offers a clarification before delving in. He tells us, "The claim is not, of course, that loving oneself is especially noble or that it reflects well upon a person's character. Rather, the claim is that love of oneself is purer than other sorts of love because it is in the case of self-love that the love is most likely to be unequivocal and unalloyed" (2004: 80). Let's follow this thread to see where it leads.

It may not be too difficult to see our way toward the purity of self-love in several of Frankfurt's specific characteristics of love. Looking at the particularity of love, I can say, in loving myself I don't love everybody who is like me. If someone came along with my good characteristics but in greater measure, I wouldn't transfer my self-love to them. (That doesn't mean I wouldn't want to be them. That's a different issue.) My love of myself can't be directed anywhere but to the particular me that I am, which is a weird way to put the point but is pretty much on target.

How about volitional necessity? This box gets pretty much checked as well. I am compelled to protect and fulfill my own interests, particularly the significant ones, not merely because I step back and choose them, but because those interests largely make up what I'm about. Here we can see the general idea of care clearly. What I care about is what's important to me, what it would be a loss to be without. I am directed toward what I care about in a way that isn't simply a matter of free and dispassionate choice. What I care about does not happen because I sit down, make a list, ponder over it, and then decide what to choose. That would distance me too much from my caring. I am *driven* toward what I care about; and in the case of myself, to be driven by what I care about and to be driven to see to my own important interests are pretty much the same thing.

The question of identification is an easy one. In self-love, I identify with the interests of the beloved because those interests just are my interests. Why? Because I am the beloved. Here there is even less distance between my identification with the interests of the beloved than there would be if the beloved is someone else. As I said earlier, I might become interested in surfing if my beloved other is, not because I want to surf, but because I am interested on their behalf. I want to participate in their interests, not by making it my own but by taking an interest in it. However, when the beloved is me, then my interests and the interests of my beloved coincide. I do take up the interests of the beloved, then, because they are the same thing as my own interests.

So far, so good. Self-love is coming off pretty pure. But here's the sticking point: disinterestedness. How can self-love be disinterested? After all, isn't self-love the most self-interested kind of love there is? Isn't that even just a matter of definition? Here Frankfurt begs to differ. He says,

> To say that a lover is disinterested means simply that he desires the good of his beloved for its own sake rather than for the sake of anything else. Self-love is disinterested in this ordinary sense, then, insofar as the person desires his own well-being for its own sake rather than for the sake of considerations that – as he himself may recognize – are extraneous to his

well-being: for instance, that his parents will be pleased
if he flourishes ... (1999: 168)

When we love ourselves, we don't do so for any reason other
than for the sake of the beloved, that is, ourselves. So isn't love
really disinterested, then?

At this point you may suspect a sleight of hand going on.
I certainly do. Frankfurt distinguishes disinterestedness from
selflessness, telling us, "Perhaps it would flirt too egregiously
with the absurd to suggest that self-love may be *selfless*. It is
entirely apposite, however, to characterize it as *disinterested*"
(2004: 82). I'm not so sure it's as apposite as all that. When we
call our love for another person disinterested, we mean that
it's not for the sake of anything else – *including ourselves*. If I say
I love someone because they give me money and praise, you
can wonder whether this is really love I'm talking about. In
love, the disinterested party is me, and the disinterest is pri-
marily, if not solely, with regard to my own personal interests.
That's the key to the "dis-" part.

If that's right, however, then Frankfurt is mistaken. And
he's mistaken not only in thinking that self-love is the purest
form of love, but in thinking that it's love *at all*, at least on his
definition. He insists on the disinterestedness of love, as well
he should. But if self-love isn't disinterested in the way we
normally think of disinterestedness, then it isn't really love.
However, if he's wrong about self-love as a form of love, where
does that leave us?

I don't think all is lost here. Whether or not we think of
what he calls self-love as a form of love, he has certainly captured an important form of self-care. Recall the three other
characteristics of love: particularity, volitional necessity and
identification with the beloved. These are all still in play.

Think of it this way. If I care for myself, then it is indeed myself that I care about. Moreover, my interests, especially my important ones, drive me in a way that's difficult to resist. Finally, I identify with my interests. Let's hang with those last two. If I care about myself, then what I care about is important to me; it moves me and I identify with its moving me. That may seem obvious, but look at it the other way around. Suppose I didn't take my caring as important. Suppose that I found myself caring about things but didn't take myself and my caring very seriously. Then I would be alienated from my own caring. It's not that I wouldn't care. I would. But I wouldn't care about the fact that I care. I wouldn't *identify* with my own caring. So if I woke up one day and found myself caring about something else, that wouldn't really matter to me. I would feel a sense of mattering and a threat of the kind of loss we discussed (way back in the first chapter) with today's object of care and no longer that sense and threat with yesterday's object of care.

What would go missing in all this, we might say, is not so much the caring but the "I" who cares, who is caught up in my own caring enough to identify myself with it. It's sort of strange to put it this way, but we might say that without identifying with my own caring I don't really care if I care. So in order to really be myself as a person who cares, my caring must be something I care about. Frankfurt himself captures a similar point when he says that, "Besides the fact that the well-being of what we love is so important to us, because of our identification of it with our own well-being, there is the separate and perhaps even deeper fact that *loving itself* is important to us" (1999: 171).

He also captures this idea from another angle when he argues that in order to love oneself one must love other things as well. This also might seem strange, but Frankfurt offers us the analogy of raising children. If you love your children, one thing you'll certainly want to do is develop their interests, and even more deeply develop their having interests in the first place: "It is not only in attempting to identify and support their children's true interests that parents convincingly manifest love for their children. They may manifest it also by doing what they can to ensure that their children *have* genuine interests" (2004: 89). Another way to put this point would be that among the tasks of parental love is to ensure that their kids develop things they care about, even if they're not the things you as a parent care about. But if that's right, then part of self-love (or self-care) would be to take it as important to develop *one's own* genuine interests – not just to find oneself caring about things (which we do as well) but also to take it upon oneself to develop things one cares about, to involve ourselves in the world in a caring way. Caring about oneself, then, does require caring about other things, and moreover it involves caring about one's own caring: tending to it, cultivating it, developing it, and perhaps reflecting on it every once in a while.

MICHEL FOUCAULT ON CARE OF THE SELF

Self-care, then, even if we don't want to call it self-love, is an important element of caring. In fact, if what we've been saying is right, self-care is necessary to give care its depth. But can we put any flesh on these bones? Can we, without falling into some kind of self-care manualizing, offer anything philosophical regarding what caring about myself might be about?

Here let's turn to the French philosopher and historian

Michel Foucault. Foucault actually published books called *The Use of Pleasure* and *The Care of the Self* (as volumes 2 and 3 respectively of *The History of Sexuality*), and a lot of folks hoped they would tell us what he thought caring for oneself should look like. But they didn't. Or better, they sort-of-didn't. To get a grip on what Foucault was and was not on about with these books, we have to get a grip on what he was and was not on about in a more general way with his writings.

Foucault is probably the most influential of the thinkers we've discussed in this book, although he's hard to categorize. His writings are taught in philosophy departments, history departments, literature departments, critical theory departments, and even women's studies departments. His writings are a kind of history, although he doesn't call them that. He called his early writings "archaeology", his middle writings "genealogy", and his later writings "ethics". His discomfort with the term "history" is that many writings that call themselves historical see history as progressive, going from a worse, more primitive time to a better, more enlightened one. He rejected that idea, not because he thought things were getting worse, but because he believed that not all change was change for the better.

In particular, Foucault thought that many of the ways we are taught to think of ourselves are constraining in deleterious ways, making us think that certain ways of being are natural or inevitable or a better reflection of what it is to be a human being when, in fact, they are a product of a contingent history – a history that could have unfolded otherwise from the way it did. If a traditional progressive history (that is, history as progress from the worse to the better) would tell us that we have become more enlightened about what humans are really like, Foucault sought to show in particular areas (for example, psychology and sexuality) that what we take for enlightened truths about the human condition are actually products of a history that has as much to do with power and politics as it does with knowledge.

Although often thought of as a pessimistic thinker – "here's how we're being constrained by our history" – he was actually quite optimistic. He once said in an interview,

> My optimism consists, rather, in saying: as long as things can be changed, fragile as they are, held together more by contingencies than by necessities, more by the arbitrary than by the obvious, more by complex but transitory historical contingency than by inevitable anthropological constraints ... You know, saying that we are much more recent than we believe is not a way of placing all the burden of our history on our shoulders. Rather, it puts within the range of work which we can do to and for ourselves the greatest possible part of what is presented to us as inaccessible. (1982: 35)

You can begin to see here how self-care might appear in Foucault's writings. If what we take to be our inescapable character or nature turns out to be the product of a contingent history, then we can be otherwise than what we have been taught we must be. At the outset of *The Use of Pleasure*, Foucault writes, "As for what motivated me, it is quite simple; I would hope that in the eyes of some people it might be sufficient in itself. It was curiosity – the only kind of curiosity, in any case, that is worth acting upon with a degree of obstinacy: not the curiosity that seeks to assimilate what it is proper for one to know, but that which enables one to get free of oneself" (1985: 8).

Foucault's history of sexuality was originally an attempt to see how we came to think of our sexuality in the ways that we do, starting from the sixteenth century. In the first volume, which serves as an introduction to the project, he suggests that we have come to think of our sexuality as the great secret that tells us who we are. We can see this, for instance, in the importance that the Catholic confessional started to accord to confessing desires, and particularly sexual desires, rather than just forbidden acts, as well as in the rise of psychoanalysis. (Having once lived in South Carolina for three decades, I can attest to the importance of ascriptions of sexuality on the part of the religious right in judging who a person is – as well as where they're likely to spend their eternal afterlife.)

After the first volume, however, Foucault thought he needed a wider historical scope in order to understand the role that sexuality had come to play in our lives, and so he started to study ancient Greek and Roman early Christian practices. As he did so, he came to believe that what we call "sexuality" is a narrower part of a wider set of practices that involve how different societies cultivated ways of developing and caring for themselves. These practices involved four elements: the determination of the ethical substance; the mode of subjection; the ethical work; and the ethical telos. (Note here that the term "ethics" refers not to a code of moral conduct but to a way of moulding oneself, of *taking care* of oneself.)

The ethical substance concerns which part of oneself the ethical work is to be done on: the soul, behaviour, emotions, and so on. The mode of subjection is the way in which a person conforms to the ethical codes current in a society: "One can, for example, practice conjugal fidelity and comply with the precept that imposes it, because one acknowledges oneself to be a member of the group that accepts it, declares adherence to it out loud, and silently preserves it as a custom. But one can practice it, too, because one regards oneself as an heir to a spiritual tradition that one has the responsibility of maintaining or reviving" (1985: 27).

The ethical work is the type of work a person does in order to mould themselves – and specifically their ethical substance – in the right ways. This can involve things like battling temptation or habituation toward a certain way of thinking or, in conjugal relationships, maintaining one's virginity before marriage. Finally, the telos is the point of all this work. Again, this can be quite varied: "conjugal fidelity can be associated with a moral conduct that aspires to an ever more complete mastery of the self; it can be a moral conduct that manifests a sudden and radical detachment vis-à-vis the world; it may strain toward a perfect tranquility of soul, a total insensitivity to the agitations of the passions, or toward a purification that will ensure salvation after death and blissful immortality" (1985: 28).

We can recognize how this schema might play out in a contemporary approach to self-care. A quick sketch of a general evangelical Christian ethics might capture the point. For evangelicals, the ethical substance is the soul (in contrast to, say, utilitarians or Kantians, for whom it is behaviour). It is the soul that is to be worked on. The mode of subjection involves the desire to have a personal relationship with Jesus. The pastor can be helpful in this, and often the pastor's words get substituted for the personal relationship with Jesus. But the point would be the motivation to cultivate that relationship itself. The ethical work is the task of bringing Jesus into one's life in an ongoing way. This involves prayer and talking to Jesus, church attendance, reflecting on the temptations one experiences to sin, and so on. And, finally, the telos is the saving of one's immortal soul.

The schema Foucault provides is far more encompassing than simply following a set of rules or guidelines that we often associate with traditional morality, such as causing the best consequences or acting in accordance with the categorical imperative. It is a whole way of being, a way a person moulds or creates themselves. Otherwise put, it is a way of taking care of oneself. It happens in different ways in different cultures, although certain cultures often present their particular ways of taking care of oneself as the only acceptable ones. What Foucault is offering here is a way of framing caring for oneself in terms of cultural practices, practices that, by our taking them up, produce us to be certain kinds of beings with certain kinds of behavioural styles and certain – often very constrained – ways of thinking about ourselves.

Now Foucault was no evangelical. Moreover, his writings on ethics focused on much earlier ways of caring for oneself. Why is this? For Foucault, as we saw, the point of his research was to get free of himself. One way to do this was to see how other people could live very different lives from the ones we live. The way it works is this. If I can recognize a very different way of people's conducting their lives from the way I do, then I am less tempted to see my own way as natural or inevitable or inescapable, as an "anthropological constraint". And that, in turn, opens the door to experimenting with other ways of being. This doesn't mean I have to copy some earlier way of being or caring for oneself. (When Foucault was asked whether he thought we should return to the forms of self-care of the ancient Greeks, he said he didn't.) It only means that by loosening the sense that my way of being is natural or inevitable or the only choices a sane or normal person can adopt, I can thereby think about other ways of cultivating my life.

To see another example of what caring for oneself may look like, let's look to Foucault's analysis of the ancient Greeks. The ethical substance he treats is what he calls *aphrodisia*, which we might broadly translate as pleasure or pleasures. Among the pleasures is what we would think of as sexual pleasure, but that's not all. Foucault also speaks of pleasures of eating and of governing the household and the body politic. In contrast to our contemporary view of sexuality as a distinct arena of pleasure (and sin, identity, and so on), for the ancient Greeks sexuality was part of a broader category subject to proper forms of self-care.

The mode of subjection for the ancient Greeks is *chresis*. This has to do with the use of pleasures. It would concern, among other things, matters of need, timeliness, and the status of those engaged in the behaviour. For example, there is timeliness in regard to the time of day, the seasons, and the time of life: "One has to keep in mind that this theme of the right time had considerable importance for the Greeks, not only as a moral problem, but also as a question of science and technique ... one was not content with knowing general prin-ciples but that one was able to know the moment when it was necessary to act and the precise manner in which to do so in terms of existing circumstances" (1985: 57–8). Many of us are familiar with the idea of *kairos* – the right moment to do some-thing. This was a central theme in the mode of subjection regarding the pleasures for the Greeks.

Foucault calls the ethical work *enkrateia*, which he describes as "an active form of self-mastery, which enables one to resist or struggle, and to achieve domination in the area of desires and pleasures" (1985: 64). The theme of struggle is important here. Rather than being what we might think of as Christian self-negation, *enkrateia* is an active form of combat in which victory can be a source of pride. If you've read Plato's *Symposium*, you've seen an example of *enkrateia*. Socrates, who is no particular looker himself, resists the sexual entreaties of the gorgeous Alcibiades, displaying *enkrateia* for the gathered guests. *Enkrateia* can be practiced in other ways as well, for instance by not gorging food at dinner or dominating a conversation with a lot of self-references.

Finally, the telos, the goal, of all this is *sophrosyne*, which is often translated as "moderation". Foucault sees it as a form of freedom. The idea here is that one is not controlled by the pleasures but is in control of them. One is master of oneself, and in particular master of one's ethical substance. This idea of mastery, Foucault points out, is particularly complex in regard to sexual relations between older men and younger men or boys. Such relations were permitted, and even at times encouraged, in ancient Greece, but their ethical character was vexed. On the one hand, the youth who was engaged in a relationship with an older man could not be the master in the relationship. This would be demeaning to the older man, who would be thought of as submissive to the youth and therefore not a master of himself. However, for the youth to be *too* submissive would also be problematic – that would show a lack of self-mastery on his part. In either case, there is the threat of unfreedom, of one party being dominated by desire for the other. For Foucault, this was a tension that ran through sexual relations between older men and youth during this period.

The ethics Foucault describes here might seem foreign to us. The idea that sexuality is just one form of a larger category of pleasure, or that in sex we should be concerned with the right time of day or the right season, or that moderation is itself a goal rather than a means for something else might seem peculiar to many of us. For Foucault, that would be the point. He doesn't mean for us to say that the ancient Greeks had it *right*, but rather that the way or ways we approach sexuality aren't the only way or ways it might be approached. This would be an encouragement toward loosening the grip of the forms of self-care that are on offer in our society – an encouragement to get free of oneself – so that we can ask ourselves in a fresh way how we would like to take care of ourselves, and can even experiment with new forms of self-care.

In an interview, Foucault was once asked how we might think about ethics in light of the historical work that he did on different forms of self-care. His response was this: "What strikes me is the fact that, in our society, art has become something that is related only to objects and not to individuals or to life. That art is something which is specialized or done by experts who are artists. But couldn't everyone's life become a work of art? Why should the lamp or the house be an art object but not our life?" (1997: 261). Recall that I said earlier that Foucault sort-of-didn't tell us what caring for oneself should look like. This is the "well, he sort-of-did" part. However, unlike your standard self-help book, Foucault wasn't interested in saying, "Here's how you do it". He didn't tell us about the seven (or five or eight) habits of successful people or recommend particular mental exercises for us to do each day or tout the health benefits of meditating at our desk. Instead, what he did was to open a door for us to walk through, showing us that the room we occupy is not the only space of self-care that there might be.

Instead of choosing between, say, a Christian lifestyle of self-abnegation and a capitalist lifestyle of self-aggrandizement, we might choose otherwise. The path this choice would lead us down would not be marked in advance. Instead of picking from a list of presented options, we might instead create our own options as we go. This prospect might seem a bit frightening to us. It's easier just to go with the flow, which is why so many people do it. But, Foucault might ask, is this really how we want to take care of ourselves? Perhaps the freedom his writings seek to offer us – not a freedom of ancient Greek self-mastery, but a freedom from particular social constraints – would allow us to ask ourselves anew who we would like to be and what shape we would like our lives to take. That, it seems, might be a form of self-care really worth having.

5

Care and vulnerability

In the previous chapters we've been discussing care as having two fundamental characteristics: importance to the person who cares and a sense of loss (grief, regret, frustration, anger, and so on) if the object of care is threatened in some way. Back in the first chapter, however, I raised the question of whether caring could happen without the second characteristic. Could someone care about something without experiencing a sense of loss if that something is harmed or dies or disappears? Or, alternatively, is it impossible, really, to care about something without the possibility of a sense of loss as part of the package? In short, does care require *vulnerability*?[1]

There are philosophies among whose goals, it seems, is to protect us against vulnerability – Buddhism and Stoicism in particular (both of which seem to be wildly popular these days as ways of coping with our fraught world). If caring and vulnerability are a package deal, this would seem to imply that Buddhists and Stoics are incapable of caring. That seems an odd thing to say. While for most of us caring and vulnerability go together, is it *necessarily* true? Are Buddhists and Stoics in fact barred from the experience of caring? The issue is more complicated to sort out than it might seem. In order to do that sorting, we'll first need to get a basic grasp on these two philosophies.

BUDDHISM

The question "What is Buddhism?" is not so much a query seeking a simple answer as an opening onto a tangle of complexities. Basic issues, such as whether Buddhism is a philosophy or a religion, are subject of long debate and disagreement. I once wrote a column for a newspaper (2014b) that was mildly critical of Buddhism, and received a number of angry comments from self-professed Buddhists claiming that I had completely misunderstood what it was all about. (I know, I also found their anger ironic.) One person told me that by referring to the Four Noble Truths – more on that in a minute – I was being too logical and missing the point of Buddhism, which was really just a feeling. Now, in a way, I can get the sense of "that Buddhist feeling", but I can't help thinking there's more to Buddhism than that.

There are, of course, many types and schools of Buddhism. There's no way to cover them all or to do justice to the subtle distinctions and discussions that have arisen in its history. (We'll briefly look at the two major schools of Buddhism in a bit.) But here's what we can do: we can look at the centrepiece of Buddhism, the Four Noble Truths, and use that to get a basic grasp of what Buddhism involves and what it might have to do with caring.

There are different translations of the Four Noble Truths, and here's one: "(1) all life is inevitably sorrowful, (2) sorrow is due to craving, (3) sorrow can only be stopped by the stopping of craving, and (4) this can be done by a course of carefully disciplined conduct, culminating in the life of concentration and meditation led by the Buddhist monk" (de Bary & Bloom: 416). The fourth Noble Truth is also given as the Eightfold Path, a path of conduct that will lead to enlightenment. The key term in this translation is "craving" (*taṇhā*), which is also sometimes translated as "attachment" or "desire". Although I'm no scholar of Pāli, the often-used translation as "desire" seems to me a bit weak. A person can desire something in the sense of wanting it without really being *attached* to it. If we're going with desire, then something like "passionate desire" might work better.

In any event, if life is inevitably sorrowful due to craving, then the task for the Buddhist is to stop the arising of craving. Following the Eightfold Path is the professed path to achieving this goal, but in order to understand that, we need to first get a grip on the Buddhist view of who and what we are. For the Buddhist, everything in the universe, including what we call our selves, is a process of constant change, arising, dissolving and becoming something else. There is no permanence in the universe, only the appearance of permanence: "All things in the universe may also be classified into five components or are mixtures of them: form and matter, sensations, perceptions, psychic dispositions or constructions, and consciousness or conscious thought" (de Bary & Bloom 1999: 416). These components are in constant flux. Although what we encounter looks as though it has permanence, it doesn't. We, and everything else, are just – to use a popular Buddhist metaphor – a wave on the ocean of Being. We arise momentarily from the ocean and so have the illusion of being a distinct self, but we're still just part of the ocean and will return to the larger body of water when we die.

Enlightenment for the Buddhist consists fundamentally

in coming to the recognition that "I" really don't exist as a separate being. That recognition is not simply an intellectual one; it has to be felt in, as it were, one's very non-being. Most of us, however, live most of our lives in the illusion that we're separate selves whose lives matter as such. When we do that, we become attached to ourselves and to what we crave. We want to continue to live, and in our living have all kinds of passionate desires that we think are important for us to satisfy. This inevitably leads to disappointment and consequently to sorrow. As one Buddhist scholar colourfully put the point in discussing the Buddhist law of dependent origination (or the chain of causation): "Ignorance is the cause of the psychic constructions, hence is caused consciousness, hence physical form, hence the six senses, hence contact, hence sensations, hence craving, hence attachment, hence becoming, hence birth, hence old age and death with all the distraction of grief and lamentation, sorrow and despair" (de Bary 1958: 101).

If, through meditation and the Eightfold Path,[2] we can incorporate into ourselves (our "selves") the truth of the universe, then we will reach *nirvāna*, a term that literally means "blowing-out". The rough idea is that the ending of craving is the ending of the illusion of a separate self. For traditional Buddhism, it may take many lifetimes to reach *nirvāna* (thus the idea of rebirth and karma), but when we reach it we step off the Wheel of Life (*samsāra*) and reach full oneness with the cosmos.

There is, however, an important distinction between the two major Buddhist schools, Theravāda and Mahāyāna. In Theravāda Buddhism, *nirvana* (*nibbana* in the Pāli canon associated with the Theravādan school) is largely an individual goal. The Buddhist seeks, perhaps over many rebirths, to be an *arhat*, a "perfect being" (*arahant* in Pali). An *arhat* is not reborn because, having lost attachment to anything in the universe, they are free to exit the Wheel of Life and its suffering. As Buddhism developed, however, many people began to see the goal of individual salvation as pretty selfish (which would seem to violate the idea of non-attachment). If someone was in a position to achieve *nirvāna*, why not assist others so they can do so? This dissatisfaction led to the emergence of Mahāyāna Buddhism ("Mahāyāna" meaning "greater vehicle"). In contrast to the figure of the *arhat*, Mahāyāna poses the figure of the *bodhisattva*, the one who puts off *nirvāna*, sacrificing ultimate salvation in order to assist others until all have achieved it.

Someone might want to ask here whether what the Buddhists are recommending is really just a form of suicide. One response the traditional Buddhist could give is that suicide will not stop a person from stepping back on to the Wheel of Life through rebirth, so it won't do the trick. Another response, perhaps a better one, is that if life is suffering, suicide is simply despair in the face of that suffering. Enlightenment is a way to rise above suffering. Although both suicide and enlightenment end a person's life, only enlightenment does so through a process of coming to terms with and therefore resonating with the nature of the universe. As one Buddhist sage puts it, "He who maintains the doctrine of Emptiness is not allured by the things of this world, because they have no basis. He is not excited by gain or dejected by loss. Fame does not dazzle him and infamy does not shame him. Scorn does not repel him, praise does not attract him. Pleasure does not please him, pain does not trouble him" (de Bary 1958: 175).

The goal of Buddhism, then, seems to involve the cessation of suffering and therefore an immunity to the vulnerability often associated with caring. But if the Buddhist cannot experience the possibility of loss that we have associated with caring, does that mean that Buddhists don't care about anything? That's the question we need to confront, after a brief foray into Stoicism.

STOICISM

"Begin each day," the Stoic Emperor Marcus Aurelius counsels himself at the outset of his famous *Meditations*, "by telling yourself: Today I shall be meeting with interference, ingratitude, insolence, disloyalty, ill-will, and selfishness – all of them due to the offender's ignorance of what is good or evil" (Marcus 1964: 45).[3] Marcus' *Meditations* are often misread by beginning students of Stoicism. They sound preachy and repetitive until you realize that he's not talking to you; he's talking to himself. The *Meditations* are a record of the struggle of a would-be Stoic trying to remind himself of the lessons of Stoicism so that he can incorporate them into his life. The exhortations are to himself, and the repetition is to remind himself of what he should already have learned and incorporated into his life. What, then, should Marcus have in mind as he goes through his day?

For the Stoic, the cosmos is a rational place. As for the Buddhists, it is a place of constant change. This change, however, is not arbitrary or capricious. It's rational. Everything that happens in the cosmos happens as it should. As Marcus reminds himself, "Providence is the source from which all things flow; and allied with it is Necessity, and the welfare of the universe. You yourself are a part of that universe; and for any one of Nature's parts, that which is assigned to it by the World-Nature or helps to keep it in being is good" (1964: 46). If the universe is a rational place, then there is no need to question or doubt or resist it. In fact, resisting it won't do you any good; it only brings you disquiet.

Stoicism is often thought of as recommending a dour fatalism, a kind of "Don't grin, but do bear it" approach to life. Although some passages in Stoic literature might lend themselves to that way of viewing Stoicism, it isn't really in keeping with the larger picture. To the contrary, their perspective can more accurately be taken as a sort of, "The universe is okay as it is, and so you can be tranquil about it".

Of course, this may seem to be all to the good, but how do we go about it? As it turns out, it's not so easy. The reason – and here we can see affinities with Buddhism – is that we often find ourselves seeking to control what actually happens in ways that the universe may or may not be open to being controlled. And that lack of ability ultimately to control things leads to disquiet, anxiety or even fear. For instance, suppose – contrary to all you know about me – I would like to go surfing. In order to be able to go surfing, however, a lot of other things have to cooperate. The weather needs to be agreeable. If a storm is raging, that won't be so good. The waves have to be up, which requires proper wind currents and so on. My car has to get me to the beach without breaking down and my friend who has just been jilted by their two-timing love interest has to refrain from calling me for support yet again. And so on. It's not that any of this will necessarily go wrong. Maybe none of it is likely to go wrong. The point is, rather, that I don't have control over any of it. And unless I'm a seriously chill surfer dude, some part of me is going to feel perturbation about all this stuff that I can't control.

What goes for surfing goes even more so for central concerns in people's lives. Will I be successful in my career? Am I a likeable person? Does that pain in my side mean I should go to the doctor? Are my children okay when they're out of my sight? Will I meet that deadline tomorrow at work, or even get to sleep tonight? What do I do about all the interference, ingratitude, insolence, disloyalty, ill-will and selfishness I'm going to run into today? We can't control any of it, and so we're often, if not constantly, in a state of somewhere between mild and staggeringly awful unrest.

The proper response to this, the Stoic tells us, is to control what we can control and let go what we cannot. As Epictetus says, "Straightaway then practice saying to every harsh appearance, You are an appearance, and in no manner what you appear to be. Then examine it by the rule which you possess, and by this first and chiefly, whether it relates to the things which are in our power or to the things which are not in our power: and if it relates to anything which is not in our power, be ready to say, that it does not concern you" (2004: 1–2). Or, with a little more pith, "Seek not that the things which happen should happen as you wish; but wish the things which happen to be as they are, and you will have a tranquil flow of life" (2004: 4).

So far, so good, but we haven't hit the hard part yet. That's the part where, in order to feel tranquil about what we can't control, we need to abandon our passions. All of them. Here are some examples of the passions we need to abandon: grief, anxiety, hope, despair, pride, elation, resentment, disgust, disappointment, boredom, excitement, craving (of course), nostalgia, sexual arousal and anger. In regard to anger, the Stoic philosopher Seneca writes, "Reason herself, who holds the reins, is only strong while she remains apart from the passions; if she mixes and befouls herself with them she becomes no longer able to restrain those whom she might once have cleared out of her path; for the mind, when once excited and shaken up, goes whither the passions drive it" (2022: 4).

That may seem difficult enough, but the task is actually harder than that. Pause a moment over this passage from Epictetus: "If you are kissing your child or wife, say that it is a human being that you are kissing, for when the wife or child dies, you will not be disturbed" (2004: 2). And in case that seems like just a slip of the pen, here's Marcus coaching himself: "Where he begs, 'Spare me the loss of my precious child,' beg rather to be delivered from the terror of losing him" (1964: 147). In fact, the Stoics admired the ancient Greek general Anaxagoras who is said to have responded to the news that his son had died in battle: "I always knew my son was mortal".

It's a challenge, yes, but it does flow from the fundamental Stoic commitment to the cosmos as a rational place. Moreover, to the degree that a person can extirpate their passions and take up the Stoic position, tranquility is likely to follow. Some may worry that rather than tranquility, the real endpoint of Stoicism is an emotional catatonia, an utter loss of involvement in life. But nothing in Stoic doctrine tells us to withdraw from our life's engagements – a point we'll return to in a bit. And if we can stay engaged with life while not being disturbed by what takes place, as the Stoic recommends, we might actually attain a certain peace that allows us to move through the world (rather than, as the Theravādan Buddhist foresees, out of it) without disturbance and without unduly disturbing others. As Marcus tells himself, "living and dying, honour and dishonor, pain and pleasure, riches and poverty, and so forth are equally the lot of good men and bad. Things like these neither elevate nor degrade; and therefore they are no more good than they are evil" (1964: 48). To take that insight into ourselves would give the lives of most of us – and certainly me – a very different character and feel from what we normally experience.

DO BUDDHISTS AND STOICS CARE? CAN THEY?

Buddhism and Stoicism overlap in important ways, but they aren't identical doctrines. For one thing, Stoics believe the cosmos is rational and well-ordered. By contrast, Buddhists don't believe the cosmos has any particular qualities. It can't be described using words. When Buddhists use words at all, they are only placeholders like Oneness or Emptiness or Nullity. Another difference is that for Stoics the goal of embracing Stoic doctrine is tranquility, while for Buddhists it is *nirvāna*, the end of the cycle of life, death and rebirth. To be sure, both Buddhists and Stoics direct a lot of their energy toward fostering equanimity in the face of suffering, illness, life disappointments and, especially, death. That equanimity, however, is only part of two distinct views of the ultimate goal of human existence.

Differences aside, however, there is an important convergence between Buddhism and Stoicism, one that leads to the question of care. Both views believe that our lives are filled with discomfort, distress, anxiety, suffering and so on; this is because of our emotional attachment to what is going on in the world. We want things to be this way or that and we feel sadness or joy or disappointment or excitement or grief or elation or relief or regret when they are this way or that – or when they might be this way or that in the future or were this way or that in the past. In order to achieve tranquility or *nirvāna*, we need ultimately to withdraw our emotional investment in the world and what happens in it.

This may seem at first glance like a recommendation for indifference to everything that happens and a consequent withdrawal from the world itself. However, it's not that simple. Both Buddhism and Stoicism commend engagement in the world and specifically engagement that is helpful to others. Both are doctrines that counsel a diminishing of self-interest and a participation in advancing the interests of others, especially their interest in either tranquility or achieving *nirvāna*. Marcus' *Meditations* were dedicated to a self-improvement that would undermine egoistic concerns; Seneca wrote numerous letters and tracts seeking to help others develop the Stoic aspects of themselves. And the Buddhist *bodhisattva* foregoes their own *nirvāna* – at least for a while – in favour of helping other less advanced students move closer to achieving it. Moreover, the Eightfold Path requires things like Right Action and Right Livelihood, which are hardly recommendations to withdraw from the world.

We might call this involvement a *solidarity* with others, if not yet a form of care. It might seem strange, however, that Stoics and Buddhists would engage in solidarity. After all, what could motivate solidarity in the absence of emotional attachment? Two things, I think. First, solidarity with others in contrast to self-absorption is a way to practice the doctrines commended by both the Buddhists and the Stoics. For most of us, an important part of our emotional attachment is to ourselves and the things we care about, in part because, as Frankfurt reminds us, we care about our caring. By focusing on the needs of others rather than ourselves, we loosen the grip of self-care and with it a good part of our emotional attachment to the world. The philosopher of ancient Greece and Rome Pierre Hadot (1995) argued that an important part of ancient philosophical practice were "spiritual exercises", mental practices that helped people incorporate particular philosophical doctrines into their lives. We saw a brief example of this with Marcus' exhortation to himself to prepare each morning for "interference, ingratitude, insolence, disloyalty, ill-will, and selfishness". The practice of solidarity could be seen, among other things, as a spiritual exercise of this type.

The other motivation for solidarity, perhaps the deeper one, is that it is itself acting in accordance with the views of Buddhists and Stoics. For the Buddhist, the self is an illusion. Everyone is simply a momentary expression of the larger whole, the One or Emptiness or Nullity. When one acts for one's own interests – or, to put it in more Buddhist terms, when "one" acts in "one's" own interests – that is forgetting that one ("one") is an illusion. Solidarity is, in its very action, a recognition that everything is a part or an aspect of a larger whole in which no particular part or aspect is privileged. For the Stoic, similarly if not identically, solidarity is an expression of the loosening of a person's sense of the importance of their own emotions. It is a recognition of the rationality of the universe over and against the emotional attachments that often take hold of a person.

Neither Stoicism nor Buddhism, then, counsel a withdrawal from the world. But still, is it caring? For both doctrines, one of the two aspects we've associated with caring has to go by the boards: the sense of loss associated with a threat to the object of care. Neither Stoicism nor Buddhism can, strictly, allow for this. Any sense of loss, whether it takes the form of sadness or anger or regret or grief or whatever, involves an emotional attachment to the world. We've seen the recommendation of Epictetus and Marcus to prepare for the death of loved ones so that you can be tranquil if they do die. Buddhism would be no different. Suffering comes from craving, in this case craving for the loved one's presence. To achieve enlightenment, you need to let go of that craving as well as all other cravings.

In the previous paragraph I stuck in the word "strictly". The reason for that is that I'm often told, especially by people interested in Buddhism, that Buddhism counsels the *opposite* of what I'm claiming here. Buddhism, they tell me, frees people up for a real fellow feeling for others. When I'm no longer caught up in my emotional needs, I'm free to feel the pain and suffering of others more fully. That, in fact, is part of my solidarity with them.

I believe that in practicing Buddhism (as well as Stoicism), a person *might* be freed in just the way these folks describe to me. However, I don't think that that is, *strictly* speaking, Buddhism. The way I would describe the difference between what they're saying and Buddhism is that while Buddhism may help them engage in others' emotional attachments by diminishing their own, the point of Buddhism is in fact the extermination of emotional attachment itself. One way to put the point would be that in Buddhist solidarity, the Buddhist secretes a distance between themselves and others, a distance that allows them to act in solidarity with them and yet not get caught up in their emotional state. The Buddhist and the Stoic do not grieve with others; rather, they act in solidarity with the grief of others.

But can there be caring without vulnerability to loss? Can a person think that something or someone is important without a sense of loss if that someone or something is threatened? This seems to me to be a possibility, albeit a strange one. In a book I once wrote (May 2017), I used the term "compassion" to describe this position. I wanted to distinguish the type of caring associated with the possibility of loss from the attitude a person might have if they're invulnerable to loss, and used the term to describe the latter. In a way, it wasn't a great choice of words, since compassion invokes the idea of passion. But it at least did the trick of separating two things: a caring that involves vulnerability to loss and something we might or might not want to call caring that is invulnerable to loss.

The Stoic and the Buddhist can, it seems to me, think of certain things as important. Clearly, a recognition of the rationality or, alternatively, the Oneness or Emptiness or Nullity of the cosmos is important to them. For the Stoic and the Buddhist, that recognition is not just worth acting on in the sense that there are lots of things worth acting on and recognizing the character of the cosmos is just one of them. For them, acting in accordance with that recognition is *more* worth doing than almost anything else. That certainly seems to me to mean that it's important to them.

So it's possible, then, that the Buddhist and the Stoic can engage in something we might want to call caring, or at least caring*. They can hold certain things to be important, and believe that it would be worse if those things were threatened in some way, without concomitantly feeling some sort of loss in the face of that threat. Fair enough. But this leaves us with a final question: *would we want it?* If this compassion is indeed a type of caring, is it a type of caring that we would want to be our type of caring?

My suspicion is that, for most of us, it is not. I don't want to say that it's wrong or mistaken or that nobody should want this. I do want to say, however, that *I* don't want it and I suspect most people don't. For most of us, caring and vulnerability to loss are a package deal. They just go together. To care about something just means for us that if what we care about – our loved ones, our significant activities, our ideals, our pets

– were threatened in some way with harm or death, we would feel grief or anger or frustration or sadness or regret. Moreover, if we didn't feel that, we would think something was wrong, either with us or with our caring.

To see that, here's an example. Let's suppose – to use a case that is too common in the US – you heard that there was a shooter that had entered an office building where a close friend of yours works. You rush over to the building to get some information. You discover that several people on the floor where they work have been killed and that the killer has just been apprehended. But you don't know who's been killed. You, of course, are anxious, probably to the point of near panic. Soon the authorities come out of the building with the names of the people who have been killed. Your friend is among them.

I don't need to tell you how you'd likely feel at that point. But let's extend the story. Suppose that someone were to come up to you and offer a drug that would immediately eliminate the grief you feel. They tell you, sincerely, that you don't *have* to feel this grief. If you take the drug, the grief will pass. And suppose they're not scamming you and they really want you to feel better. Do you take the drug?

For most of us, the answer is, of course not. It's not that you *want* to feel the grief you're feeling. That would misdescribe the situation. Rather, it's that your grief is part of your caring. To get rid of the grief would feel like a diminishing of the caring itself. Caring and vulnerability, again for most (but not necessarily all) of us, go together. On the one hand, we don't *want* to experience grief or anger or regret or whatever; these are all deeply unpleasant emotions. On the other hand, we do want to be the kind of people who, under the right circumstances, are vulnerable to experiencing them. And those circumstances are the ones that involve caring.

Conclusion

There are many things, aside from surfing, that we may care about, and many ways of caring. We care about people, ideals, places, sports, activities and non-human animals. Within these categories, and undoubtedly others, we have particular objects of care. We have friends, loved ones and close acquaintances. We care about justice or equality or decency or duty or happiness or some combination of these. We might care about Peru or England or Japan or Brunei or Sierra Leone or Norway. Basketball, hockey, curling, handball and baseball are all objects of care for many. And we care about our pets or our environment or the Brazilian rain forest or the continued existence of Siberian tigers.

Moreover, across these particular objects of care are different kinds of caring: love, concern, rooting (in the case of sports teams), enjoyment, pride, protectiveness, and the various forms of engagement that these and other types of care involve.

The objects and types of care listed here – along with many others you undoubtedly thought of while reading these – although extensive, don't capture the most significant aspect of care. Care is what ties us most profoundly to the world.

It is our way of binding ourselves to the world through our passionate engagement with particular things in particular ways. It reveals who we are by revealing our most important relationships with what is outside of us.

And even to use the phrase "outside of us" doesn't capture the pervasiveness of the world through our caring. In caring, not only do we reach out both emotionally and behaviourally to the world; the world reaches into us. Our caring happens out there, to be sure. But it also happens in here, where my thoughts and my emotions are born and nourished. It is the profoundest form of commerce between me and the world in which my life takes place. Were there no caring, both me and the world would be diminished, impoverished in numerous ways.

This book has been only an introduction to the philosophy of caring. But the philosophy of caring is, in many ways, itself only in its infancy. Frankfurt's writings on care date from the early 1980s, as does care ethics. Peter Singer's seminal book on animal rights, *Animal Liberation*, that launched so much focus on and caring about non-human animals, was published in 1975. Self-care has been an object of philosophical reflection since before Aristotle, but Frankfurt's and Foucault's important discussions of it are from the 1980s, 1990s and 2000s. There is, no doubt, much more to be thought and said about this aspect of our lives.

Philosophy has as its task to reflect on the most significant questions that occupy us, those that do not, like the sciences, have an agreed upon method of resolution. How should we act? What is knowledge? How should our social and political relations be arranged? What is the nature of reality? Too often, professional philosophers – like other professional academics – devote themselves to details of the field whose bearing on these and other questions is, to be delicate, a tad unclear. When philosophers do hold true to their task, however, they still, even after several thousand years, find things worth saying and worth our hearing.

What has been said in the past 40 or so years about care, even where there has been disagreement (as between Frankfurt and Jaworska), has opened up and deepened ways of thinking about the nexus between us and the world. Going forward, philosophy could do a lot worse than to continue these lines of reflection (and those we haven't considered here, especially in care ethics), extending our understanding of how we and the world engage and mould each other through the process and activity of our caring.

Notes

1. Surfers can be serious about preserving the surfing environment. In 2006, surfers worked alongside indigenous groups to prevent a toll road from being built in southern California. The toll road would have run parallel to the creek bed that feeds a stretch of beach called the Trestles, which is an internationally known surfing area. The indigenous groups were opposing the road because they had a 9,600-year-old burial ground right there, while the surfers were opposing it because it would mess up the wave patterns. They combined efforts and, in 2008, they won. For this story, see Gilio-Whitaker (2019: 132–5). Thanks to Del McWhorter for the reference.
2. I have had several suggestions for alternatives, mostly centring around things like "adult children" and "grown kids", which strike me as having the paradoxical sound of something like "jumbo shrimp". One friend, who is gratefully childless, suggested "spawn".
3. Some studies suggest that the impact of a mass shooting on those who are not involved lasts only a few days: see https://www.washingtonpost.com/outlook/2022/05/26/uvalde-school-shooting-emotions-guns/.
4. Some folks who have studied Martin Heidegger's *Being and*

Time might ask whether that work should be the touchstone for thinking about the nature of caring. However, Heidegger's discussion of care (in German, *sorge*) is different from the approach taken here. For Heidegger, care is coextensive with our being-in-the-world. It is our way of being-in-the-world. So it concerns not only the things that are important to us, but ways of being that we just go along with. As Heidegger puts it in his usual lucid prose, "The formally existential totality of Dasein's ontological structural whole must therefore be grasped in the following structure: the Being of Dasein means ahead-of-itself-Being-already-in-(the-world) as Being-alongside (entities encountered within-the-world). This Being fills in the signification of the term 'care' [*sorge*], which is used in a purely ontologicoexistential manner" (Heidegger 1962: 237).

5. In the actual example Frankfurt uses, the person does still care about the concert. He doesn't want to give up his desire to go to the concert, because the music is important to him. Rather, he cares *more* about helping his friend. I've eliminated that complication just to make the example a bit simpler. But it shows that we can sometimes care about things that we can't commit to at a particular moment because of other things we care about more.

6. David Shoemaker (2003) also links caring with emotion in an interesting discussion of free will. He does not, however, detail his discussion of emotion in the way Jaworska does.

2.   CARE ETHICS

1. Many of Kohlberg's papers have been collected in the two volumes entitled *Essays on Moral Development* (1981/84).

2. Perhaps the most popular account of utilitarianism is John Stuart Mill's aptly named *Utilitarianism*. One place to find it is here: https://www.gutenberg.org/files/11224/11224-h/11224-h.htm.

3. In what follows we'll focus, for the sake of concision, mostly on the work of two prominent care ethicists, Joan Tronto

and Virginia Held. In her book *The Ethics of Care* (2006), Held offers a long list of care ethics works in chronological order, for those who are interested in following up the ideas in this chapter; see footnote 69 on pp. 173–4. A couple more recent books on care are Care Collective (2020) and Dowling (2022).

4. I'm going to use the term "ethics" and the term "morality" pretty interchangeably here. In philosophy, the two are sometimes distinguished. Morality is often seen as having to do with our obligations to others whereas ethics is about the question of how we should live. For our purposes, this distinction doesn't really matter, and anyway care ethics throws the distinction into disarray.

5. For a lively account of the contributions of these women, see Lipscomb (2021).

6. If I were to date the moment of its integration, I would go, perhaps a bit arbitrarily, with Bernard Williams' *Ethics and the Limits of Philosophy* (1985).

7. There are a zillion translations of the *Nichomachean Ethics*. Here's one: http://classics.mit.edu/Aristotle/nicomachaen.html.

8. The philosopher Rosalind Hursthouse has tried to show how virtue ethics can navigate through particular moral dilemmas; see Hursthouse (1999), especially chapters 2 and 3.

9. In most cases rather than all cases because there can be extremist movements that, in order to preserve a more or less democratic order, must be stopped. (Yes, tolerance does not need to include tolerating the intolerant.) Unfortunately for us, one of those extremist movements seems to have taken hold of a major political party in the US.

10. For those who want to read more about specific political recommendations within a care ethical approach, here are a few suggestions. For social justice, Slote (2007: ch. 6); for global politics, Robinson (1999: esp chs 6 and 7); for caring and public policy, White (2000). Held also has discussions of health care, law, and international relations in *The Ethics of Care*.

3.   CARE AND THE NON-HUMAN

1. I know. This sentence was uncalled for. But the opening was there and, really, it was pretty hard to avoid.
2. One balker is the law professor Richard Epstein; see Epstein (2002).
3. The most famous moral individualist is Peter Singer, whose book *Animal Liberation* (1975) is the founding text for contemporary movements in animal rights. It will appear in the next section. For an interesting and nuanced response to moral individualism, you could read Anderson (2005).
4. He comments further, "If we think it is wrong to treat a human in a certain way, because the human has certain characteristics, *and a particular non-human animal also has those characteristics*, then consistency requires that we also object to treating the non-human animal in that way." (1990: 175, emphasis added).
5. Singer holds a particularly controversial position on this. He has debated this issue with disability rights theorists; see, for example, New York Times (1999).
6. For my own part, I think moral individualism is about half right. For those of you who have too much free time on your hands and are vexed about the issue, you could peruse my article, May (2014a).
7. See https://thehumaneleague.org/article/animal-slaughter (accessed 5 July 2022). The same number comes up with this website: https://www.animalmatters.org/facts/farm/ (accessed 5 July 2022).
8. See https://www.discovermagazine.com/planet-earth/ 64-spain-gives-great-apes-legal-rights (accessed 5 July 2022).
9. Lori Gruen's concept of "entangled empathy" argues for an interactive caring rather than a broad philosophical caring like utilitarianism or deontology as an approach to our moral relationship to non-human animals; see Gruen (2020).
10. Chris Grau points out that it's possible that I could prefer the ecosystem aside from its qualities if, say, I grew up with it and came to love it, which is a good point. I'm grateful to

him for discussion of this issue, and in return cite his own article (2004) where he gets into the thickets of concepts like intrinsic value, final value, unique value, and so on.

11. Here's a recent addition to the list: artificial intelligence. Can a person care about AI? The recent movie *Her* seems to suggest that one can, although I find that kind of creepy. If I thought I was communicating with a person that I cared about and it turned out to be a computer program, I would probably develop real doubts about, well, lots of things. And if I found myself caring about something I knew was a program, those doubts would be resolved, but not in a good way.

4. CARING FOR OURSELVES

1. Actually, depending on sales, I might wind up doing it anyway.
2. My book *A Decent Life* (2019) tries to offer a different, less demanding, view of morality.
3. There are some really good books on happiness that offer a nuanced account of the idea. For instance, Haybron (2008), which sees happiness as a convergence of several factors, which he calls attunement, engagement and endorsement. But even so, I think self-care is a wider concept than happiness.

5. CARE AND VULNERABILITY

1. Many of the themes of this chapter, and especially vulnerability and invulnerability, are discussed in greater detail in my book, *A Fragile Life* (2017). In addition to Buddhism and Stoicism, I threw in Daoism and Epicureanism for good measure.
2. Right View, Right Intention, Right Speech, Right Action, Right Livelihood, Right Effort, Right Mindfulness, Right Concentration.
3. This passage opens the second book of the *Meditations*. In the first book, he thanks just about everyone in creation for just about everything that's ever happened to him, so this passage opens the meditations themselves.

References

Anderson, E. (2005). "Animal rights and the values of a nonhuman life". In C. Sunstein & M. Nussbaum (eds), *Animal Rights: Current Debates and New Directions*. Oxford: Oxford University Press.

Aristotle (n.d.). *Nichomachean Ethics*. Trans. W. D. Ross. The Internet Classics Archive. http://classics.mit.edu/Aristotle/nicomachaen.html.

Care Collective (2020). *The Care Manifesto: The Politics of Interdependence*. New York: Verso.

de Bary, T. (ed.) (1958). *Sources of Indian Tradition*. New York: Columbia University Press.

de Bary, T. & I. Bloom (comp.) (1999). *Sources of the Chinese Tradition, Volume 1: From Earliest Times to 1600*. Second edition. New York: Columbia University Press.

Dowling, E. (2022). *The Care Crisis: What Caused it and How Can We End it?* New York: Verso.

Epictetus (2004). *Enchiridion*. Trans. G. Long. Mineola, NY: Dover.

Epstein, R. (2002). "Animals as objects, or subjects, of rights". John M. Olin Law and Economics Working Paper No. 171, University of Chicago. https://chicagounbound.uchicago.edu/cgi/viewcontent.cgi?article=1052&context=law_and_economics.

Fisher, B. & J. Tronto (1991). "Toward a feminist theory of care". In E. Abel & M. Nelson (eds), *Crisis of Care: Work and Identity in Women's Lives*. New York: SUNY Press.

Foucaut, M. (1982). "Is it really important to think? An interview". Trans T. Keenan. *Philosophy and Social Criticism* 9(1): 31–40. https://monoskop.org/images/1/15/Foucault_Michel_1981_1982_Is_It_Really_Important_to_Think_An_Interview.pdf.

Foucault, M. (1985). *The Use of Pleasure: Volume 2 of the History of Sexuality*. Trans. R. Hurley. New York: Random House.

Foucault, M. (1997). "On the genealogy of ethics: an overview of work in progress". *Ethics: Subjectivity and Truth*. New York: The New Press.

Francione, G. (2004). "Animals – property or persons?". Rutgers Law School Faculty Papers 21. https://core.ac.uk/download/pdf/76622908.pdf.

Frankfurt, H. (1982). "The importance of what we care about". *Synthese* 53(2): 257–72.

Frankfurt, H. (1999). "On caring". In *Necessity, Volition, and Love*. Cambridge: Cambridge University Press.

Frankfurt, H. (2004). *The Reasons of Love*. Princeton, NJ: Princeton University Press.

Gilio-Whitaker, D. (2019). *As Long as Grass Grows: The Indigenous Fight for Environmental Justice from Colonization to Standing Rock*. Boston, MA: Beacon Press.

Gilligan, C. (1982). *In A Different Voice*. Cambridge, MA: Harvard University Press.

Goldie, P. (2000). *The Emotions: A Philosophical Exploration*. Oxford: Oxford University Press.

Grau, C. (2004). "Irreplaceability and unique value". *Philosophical Topics* 32(1/2): 111–29.

Grau, C. (2010). "Love and history". *Southern Journal of Philosophy* 48(3): 246–71.

Gruen, L. (2020). "What motivates us to change what we eat?" *The Philosopher* 108(1).

Hadot, P. (1995). "Spiritual exercises". In A. Davidson (ed.), *Philosophy as a Way of Life: Spiritual Exercises from Socrates to Foucault*. Trans. M. Chase. Oxford: Blackwell.

Haybron, D. (2008). *The Pursuit of Unhappiness: The Elusive Psychology of Well-Being*. Oxford: Oxford University Press.

Heidegger, M. (1962). *Being and Time*. Trans. J. Macquarrie & E. Robison. Oxford: Blackwell.

Held, V. (2006). *The Ethics of Care: Personal, Political, and Global*. Oxford: Oxford University Press.

Helm, B. (2010). *Love, Friendship, and the Self: Intimacy, Identification, and the Social Nature of Persons*. Oxford: Oxford University Press.

Hursthouse, R. (1999). *On Virtue Ethics*. Oxford: Oxford University Press.

Jaworska, A. (2007). "Caring and internality". *Philosophy and Phenomenological Research* 74(3): 529–68.

Jaworska, A. & M. Wonderly (2020). "Love and caring". In C. Grau & A. Smuts (eds), *Oxford Handbook of the Philosophy of Love*. Oxford: Oxford University Press.

Jollimore, T. (2011). *Love's Vision*. Princeton, NJ: Princeton University Press.

Kant, I. (1997). *Groundwork of the Metaphysics of Morals*. Trans. M. Gregor. Cambridge: Cambridge University Press.

Kelly, C. (2013). "Building bridges with accessible care: disability studies, feminist care scholarship, and beyond". *Hypatia* 28(4): 789–90.

Kittay, E. (1999). *Love's Labor: An Essay on Women, Equality, and Dependency*. New York: Routledge.

Kohlberg, L. (1981). *The Philosophy of Moral Development: Moral Stages and the Idea of Justice. Essays on Moral Development Volume 1*. New York: Harper & Row.

Kohlberg, L. (1984). *The Psychology of Moral Development: The Nature and Validity of Moral Stages. Essays on Moral Development Volume 2*. New York: Harper & Row.

Kolodny, N. (2003). "Love as valuing a relationship". *Philosophical Review* 112(4): 135–89.

Lipscomb, B. (2021). *The Women Are Up to Something: How Elizabeth Anscombe, Philippa Foot, Mary Midgley, and Iris Murdoch Revolutionized Ethics*. Oxford: Oxford University Press.

Marcus Aurelius (1964). *Meditations*. Trans. M. Staniforth. London: Penguin.

May, T. (2014a). "Moral individualism, moral relationalism, and obligations to non-human animals". *Journal of Applied Philosophy* 31(2): 155–68.

May, T. (2014b). "Against invulnerability". *New York Times*, The Stone blog, 27 December. https://archive.nytimes.com/opinionator. blogs.nytimes.com/2014/12/27/against-invulnerability/.

May, T. (2017). *A Fragile Life: Accepting Our Vulnerability*. Chicago, IL: University of Chicago Press.

May, T. (2019). *A Decent Life: Morality For the Rest of Us*. Chicago, IL: University of Chicago Press.

McGinnis, J. (1999). *The Miracle of Castel di Sangro*. Boston, MA: Little, Brown.

New York Times (1999). "Princeton bioethics professor debates views on disability and euthanasia". *New York Times*, 13 October.

https://www.nytimes.com/1999/10/13/nyregion/princeton-bioethics-professor-debates-views-on-disability-and-euthanasia.html.

Nozick, R. (1989). "Love's bond". In *The Examined Life: Philosophical Meditations*, 68–86. New York: Simon & Schuster.

Rachels, J. (1990). *Created From Animals: The Moral Implications of Darwinism*. Oxford: Oxford University Press.

Robinson, F. (1999). *Globalizing Care: Ethics, Feminist Theory, and International Relations*. Boulder, CO: Westview.

Seneca (2022). *On Anger*. Book 1, Section 7. Trans. J. Basore. http://www.sophia-project.org/uploads/1/3/9/5/13955288/seneca_anger.pdf.

Shoemaker, D. (2003). "Caring, identification, and agency". *Ethics* 114: 88–118.

Singer, P. (1972). "Famine, affluence, and morality". *Philosophy and Public Affairs* 1(3): 229–43.

Singer. P. (1975). *Animal Liberation: A New Ethics for Our Treatment of Animals*. New York: Random House.

Slote, M. (2007). *The Ethics of Care and Empathy*. New York: Routledge.

Tronto, J. (1993). *Moral Boundaries: A Political Argument for an Ethic of Care*. New York: Routledge.

Velleman, D. (1999). "Love as a moral emotion". *Ethics* 109(2): 338–74.

White, J. (2000). *Democracy, Justice, and the Welfare State: Reconstructing Public Care*. University Park, PA: Penn State University Press.

Williams, B. (1981). "Persons, character, and morality". In *Moral Luck: Philosophical Papers 1973–1980*. Cambridge: Cambridge University Press.

Ziblatt, D. & S. Levitsky (2018). *How Democracies Die*. New York: Crown.

Index